D0930534

The Delights of TURKEY

Also by EDOUARD RODITI

Oscar Wilde (critical guidebook)

The Delights of TURKEY

TWENTY TALES

Edouard Roditi

A New Directions Book

Copyright © 1972, 1973, 1977 by Edouard Roditi
Copyright © 1967, 1969 by Playboy

All rights reserved. Except for brief passages quoted in a newspaper, magazine, radio, or television review, no part of this book may be reproduced in any form or by any means, electronic or mechanical, including photocopying and recording, or by any information storage and retrieval system, without permission in writing from the Publisher.

Manufactured in the United States of America
First published clothbound and as New Directions Paperbook 445 in 1977
Published simultaneously in Canada by McClelland & Stewart, Ltd.

Library of Congress Cataloging in Publication Data

Roditi, Edouard.
    The delights of Turkey.
    (A New Directions Book)
    CONTENTS: A city built on seven hills: The magic carpet. An ailment that spread fast and far. The ghost Popo. The boulissa's pilgrimage. The imprisoned princess.—The chronicles of Bok Köy: Kurd Hikmet's harem. Introducing Achmet Hodja. How the office of eunuch of the bathrobe became hereditary. Why Napoleon erected the obelisk in the center of his Capital. The turd that was as big as a house.—Orient express: Mademoiselle Blanche. A patriotic girl. The sultan's little harum-scarum. A meek wolf among savage lambs. The angel of death. [etc.]
    I. Title.
PZ4.R6915De [PS3535.O338]   813'.5'2   77–9588
ISBN 0–8112–0669–6
ISBN 0–8112–0670–x pbk.

New Directions Books are published for James Laughlin
by New Directions Publishing Corporation,
333 Sixth Avenue, New York 10014

ACKNOWLEDGMENTS

Several of these stories have been published in one or another of the following periodicals: *Playboy, New Directions in Prose and Poetry, The Literary Review, The Expatriate Review, Present Tense, Gay Sunshine, The Virginia Woolf Quarterly, Bastard Angel,* and *Key West Arts Review.* "The Boulissa's Pilgrimage," after first appearing in the original English text in *The Literary Review,* was moreover published in French in *L'Arche,* in Paris, and in Spanish in *Papeles de Son Armadans,* the remarkable literary review edited in Palma de Mallorca by Don Camilo José Cela of the Royal Academy of Spain.

The stories first published in *Playboy* ("How the Office of Eunuch of the Bathrobe Became Hereditary," "Why Napoleon Erected the Obelisk in the Center of His Capital," and "A Meek Wolf among Savage Lambs") appeared as "Ribald Classics," but are nevertheless original stories, based on popular Turkish folklore of the same general nature as the anonymous tales about Karagöz or Nasreddin Hodja.

To the editors and publishers of all the above-mentioned periodicals, thanks are now due for permission to reprint these stories here.

EDOUARD RODITI

CONTENTS

I

A CITY BUILT ON
SEVEN HILLS

THE MAGIC CARPET

This isn't a tale about a bird that could fly beneath the waves of the sea, nor about a fish that swam above the clouds; nor again about a man endowed by Allah with extraordinary but quite useless gifts, nor about a fool who could never be wrong. If you wish to hear all about the warriors who slept a hundred years in a cave, you must go elsewhere, and I'm certainly not the storyteller who will relate to you today the adventures of a shipwrecked sailor who found on a desert isle a gigantic bird that carried him home on its wing. I'm a plain man telling you plain tales, and this one is about a magic carpet that couldn't even fly.

Many, many years ago, a conquered Tatar Khan from the wild steppes of Turkestan, beyond the Caspian Sea, was forced to give his daughter in marriage to our victorious Sultan, a great ruler indeed, may his soul rest in peace! She was a Princess of unique beauty according to the strange tastes of her slit-eyed race, whose women enjoy unusual freedom, riding the steppes with their menfolk all day and even hunting, with falcons on their wrists, in the precipitous mountain ranges that divide their lands from the vast empire administered by the Mandarins of the court of Peking. Besides, she had always been the favorite daughter of the Khan, her father.

In the harem of the Ruler of All the Faithful, in our great city of Stamboul that is built on seven hills and is destined to remain, for at least a thousand years, the capital of the civilized world, this unfortunate Princess never became accustomed to the rigors of her otherwise enviable fate. Each day, as she gazed from her latticed window in the Palace of Top Kapu Sarai across the blue waters of the Sea of Marmara and the Bosphorus to the hills of the Asiatic shore, she could see two continents nearly meet, like the lips of timid young lovers who dare not kiss; but she was then tortured by memories of sterner Asian landscapes that were hidden far beyond these lovely hills, vast plains and rugged mountains that spoke to her broken heart in the words of her own race. For her marriage to our Sultan had not been happy. Instead of becoming the companion, as she had been brought up in her childhood to expect, of some wild Prince of her own race with whom she would live and ride and hunt as if nothing, in the daytime, distinguished her at all from her Lord and Master, she was now forced to sulk all day in a splendid harem with hundreds of other idle wives and concubines. As for her nights, she spent most of them in utter solitude while the Sultan drank wine and ate lobsters as if he were an Infidel, surrounded by Armenian and Bedouin dancing girls who obeyed his slightest whim, like expensive prostitutes who have no pride and who entertain all who come their way in the luxurious houses of ill fame for which Paris is famous.

This Tatar Princess with whose sad fate we are now concerned therefore decided, one day, to while away the rigors of her splendid exile by weaving with her own hands the most beautiful gold-threaded carpet that had ever yet been made according to the traditional patterns of her own tribe. Instead of being a prayer rug depicting the *mihrab* that indicates to us, in our mosques, the direction in which we must turn toward Mecca

4

whenever we pray, as do most of the fine carpets woven in our own provinces of Eastern Anatolia, this particular carpet's pattern was that of a paradisiac garden, with a great pomegranate tree spreading its branches, loaded with rich red fruit, all over the central part, where flowers and herbs were depicted all around the tree; and the border of the carpet was conceived in a geometrical pattern, originally brought to these Sogdian and Bactrian marches of Iskender Al-Akbar's empire by the Greek artisans who accompanied his armies, but cunningly devised here so as to repeat in its mazelike design all the colors of the tree and of the flowers and shrubs of the garden of the central pattern.

For many years, the Princess persevered day after day in her despondency at this strange task that was her only solace, so unsuited to the delicate hands of the Queen of Queens in the harem of one of our Sultans. When at last the carpet was finished, all the other ladies of the Sultan's great harem were dazzled by its complex beauty. But the Tatar Princess knew that she had now lost what little soul the Prophet allows a woman to have. All her hopes, her ability to love and to dream, all her spiritual insights into the mysteries of life and death, had gone into the weaving of the carpet. She therefore prepared herself to die without ever seeing her distant homeland again. Hanging the wonderful carpet on the tiled wall of her private apartment, where she could contemplate it at all hours from her deathbed, she withdrew from the secluded world of the Sultan's many wives and concubines and awaited the death that had become her only hope, as if her last hour were indeed a secret tryst with a lover. But as she lay dying, she suddenly wished, with her last strength and consciousness, that her gold-threaded carpet would some day fall into the hands of a Prince who, under more favorable circumstances, might have understood and fulfilled her hopes and ideals and been willing to allow her the kind of modestly devoted freedom that the married women of her race all enjoy and for which she now pined.

Now it came to pass, over a hundred years after the death of our unfortunate Princess, that the harems of our Sultans fell upon evil days. A series of profligate Rulers of All the Faithful had so depleted, with their extravagances and their disastrous wars, the Imperial Treasury, that the wives and concubines of the ruling Sultan's harem were often forced to sell, to heretical Persians or to Infidel Greek, Armenian, or Jewish merchants from the Great Covered Bazaar, through the good offices of the Palace's eunuchs, many of the Imperial treasures that no true Sunni Moslem would handle; with these clandestine sales, the ladies of the harem were able to procure enough money for the bare necessities of their cloistered life, for their wearing apparel and for the kohl and henna and other cosmetics without which they dared not appear, when summoned, in the presence of their Lord and Master.

One day, this ancient gold-threaded carpet, its gold all tarnished with age, chanced to be discovered in a chest in the abandoned apartment of a recently deceased Sultana Walideh, the dowager mother of an already deceased Sultan. There the precious carpet had been forgotten, it seemed, throughout a whole series of reigns of our Sultans.

An Armenian eunuch, one Krikor Karapetian who was a native of a village on the shores of Lake Van, was entrusted forthwith with the sale of this useless carpet and with the purchase of some sorely needed toiletries. Like all good Armenians, Krikor had numerous relatives who depended on his position in the Sultan's household for occasional assistance in earning their livelihood. Among these relatives was a carpet dealer, one Kevork Ekmekjian, who bought the carpet from the eunuch Krikor for a song, without haggling over the price, the eunuch having been, that day, unusually modest in his demands.

Kevork Ekmekjian carried on his business in a shop in the Covered Bazaar, close to the entrance where one accedes to its galleries through the courtyard of the Nouri Osmanyeh Mosque. Many foreign tourists and dealers flocked to him for souvenirs and rarities, for Kevork spoke fluently half a dozen of the languages of the Infidels, having accompanied in his youth an uncle

6

who was a great merchant on this hook-nosed magnate's annual trips to the fairs in Nijni Novgorod and Leipzig, in Milano, Paris, and Chicago. A few days later, a French antique dealer thus chanced to come by Kevork's shop in the Covered Bazaar, saw the gold-threaded carpet, haggled over the price, drank several cups of free coffee with Kevork, then agreed at long last to buy the carpet for considerably less than had originally been asked, though still leaving Kevork a handsome profit. The Frenchman paid for the carpet and took it back forthwith, under his arm, to his room in the Pera Palace Hotel, on the hill that rises on the far side of the Golden Horn. During the night, the carpet vanished mysteriously from the Frenchman's room. He presumed, of course, that it had been stolen. He therefore complained the next morning to the manager of the hotel, a Frenchman too, since the Pera Palace still belonged, in those days, to the *Compagnie Internationale des Wagons-Lits et des Grands Express Européens,* which had built it. But no trace of a thief could be found by the management or by the Austrian fingerprint experts of our police, so the whole matter was left at that when the French dealer boarded the Orient Express, a few days later, bound for his native Paris.

Several months went by, during which Kevork Ekmekjian made his annual trip to Iran, to attend the great carpet sales in Tabriz and Isfahan, in Shiraz, Hamadan, Meshed, and Teheran, where the villagers and the Yuruk nomads from all over Iran and the Turkish-speaking provinces of the Muscovites offer their wares. Kevork purchased wisely, that year, but quite extensively too, noting in a book that he carried in his pocket the exact description of each item contained in each bale that he acquired.

On his return to Stamboul, he began to unpack and to check these bales as they arrived, one after the other, by caravan as far as Haydar Pasha, where the station has now been built, on the Asiatic shore opposite our city, for the railroad that serves ham in its restaurant on wheels to the Infidel tourists and their unveiled wives when they travel from here to Cairo and to Baghdad. From Haydar Pasha, these bales of carpets were then transported by boat across the strait and unloaded on the docks of Eminönü, on the Stamboul shore of the Golden Horn. Suddenly, in one of these bales, Kevork one day came across a Samarkand carpet that he had not listed in his book, an exact replica, if he remembered right, of the one that he had purchased some months earlier from the Sultan's Palace and then sold almost immediately to his Parisian customer. Puzzled, Kevork decided to list the carpet, for the time being, in the inventory of his stock, but not to offer it for sale until he had received from Tabriz, where he had purchased this particular bale, a reply to his inquiry, which he sent off that day, about the error which might have occurred in the packing of this shipment. The Iranian broker through whose good offices he had purchased this bale in Tabriz answered Kevork's letter immediately, though it was some months before his reply reached Stamboul. The broker professed total ignorance of the very existence of so rare and unusual a rug, affirming that it would certainly have caused a sensation, had it ever appeared for sale on the Tabriz market, in these days of inferior mass-produced wares that are made and sold mainly for export to the lands of the Infidels rather than for use in decent Moslem homes. Kevork Ekmekjian then decided to offer the gold-threaded carpet for sale again, since fate seemed to have decided that he was destined, should it even be the one which he had already sold, to make quite unusual profits on its sale.

The first customer who now saw the rug was a Swiss, the owner of a famous carpet store on the Bahnhofstrasse in Zurich. Again, there was some haggling over the price before the two merchants reached agreement. Again the gold-threaded carpet disappeared, as mysteriously as the first time, that very night, from the Swiss purchaser's room, this time in the Büyuk Londra Hotel. Again, no trace of a thief could be found.

About a year later, Kevork Ekmekjian called one day on a poor relative who lived close to the Armenian Church in Psamattia. This is an Armenian neighborhood, situated above the fields and vegetable gardens that one now finds where the Navy of the

Byzantine Emperors once had their harbor and docks in Langna, on the shore of the Sea of Marmara, on the far side of the Old City, beyond the Aksarai quarter and the ancient mosque of Davoud Pasha, which is reputed to have been first built, long before Sultan Mehmet the Conqueror stormed the city, for the many Moslem merchants who had already settled, for business reasons, in the Byzantine capital. It was to this poor relative, an uncle on his mother's side and an old man who, being a native of the region of Erzurum, was versed in all the skills of ancient times, that Kevork generally gave, for necessary repairs, his most precious antique rugs. But the old man had now been ill for some time, and delays had occurred in his deliveries of a number of rare rugs that he had agreed to repair. Kevork therefore decided on the spur of the moment to visit him in order to see with his own eyes whether the old man's failing strength was likely to allow him to resume work, to finish the tasks already entrusted to him, and perhaps even accept some new tasks. Much to his surprise, Kevork found the old man at work, seated beneath his oil lamp, with a whole pile of rugs that he had already mended neatly folded beside him. He was even now at work mending what he cheerfully said was the last rug that his nephew had sent him, only two or three days ago, for urgent repairs. Kevork was scarcely able to believe his own eyes when he recognized, unfolded on the old man's lap as he sat there on the floor, the precious gold-threaded Samarkand rug which he had already sold twice.

"But where did you find this carpet, Uncle Agop?"

"Don't you remember sending it to me, only last week? One of the boys who works for you in the bazaar brought it to me and asked me to mend it immediately."

"Which one of the boys?"

"I had never seen him before, a new lad who neglected to tell me his name, tall and dark, with the slit eyes of those Turkmenian nomads who used to come and sell their wares in the marketplace of Erzurum. But he distinctly told me that you had sent him and that I was to expect your visit today. That's why I hastened to do the job at once, and I'll have finished it in only a couple of minutes, so just sit down and wait, while my wife prepares us a couple of cups of coffee."

Kevork was utterly mystified, but sat and waited until the old man had finished binding the border of the gold-threaded carpet where it was slightly worn. Kevork then took it back with him, an hour later, to his shop in the Covered Bazaar, but cautiously refrained from showing it again to any customers in the course of the next few months, just in case someone might come and claim it as his own rightful property, which it well might be.

But one day a new customer wandered into Kevork's store, to which he appeared to have been led by one of the innumerable touts of the bazaar, a tall and dark-haired boy with slit eyes, wearing a strange caftan such as one still sees a few nomad Turkmenian or Tatar tribesmen wear in the most distant provinces of Eastern Anatolia. The customer himself was a tall young man from America, fair-haired and ruddy-complexioned, but with the high cheekbones and the almost slit eyes of those Americans from the West who, in their incomprehensible movies about legendary bandits and cattle thieves, generally claim to be descended, on their mother's side, from a Red Indian Princess. Kevork was immediately struck by some obscure resemblance between the American and the tout who had brought him to his shop, but began at once to show his new customer a selection of the cheap and gaudy Sarouks that usually appeal to the unschooled tastes of Americans. But this boy, who seemed to be scarcely older than twenty, displayed no interest at all in such mediocre examples of Turkish art and began to ask whether he might be shown some more unusual carpets, naming specifically the rugs of Baku and Samarkand and some rare nomad rugs that appear ever less frequently on the market. Puzzled, Kevork retired to his storeroom to select a few such carpets, but first sent out one of his assistants to order two cups of coffee from a neighboring coffeehouse, as one always does when entertaining a distinguished customer.

When Kevork returned from his storeroom with a selection

of rare rugs, he found the American staring, as if entranced, at the mysterious gold-threaded rug. But Kevork had only just set it aside in his storeroom, deeming it unsuitable for a customer whom he believed to be too young, too ignorant, or too poor to appreciate and purchase such a treasure. Yet it now lay here, spread on the floor at the American's feet. Kevork could only exclaim:

"Who brought you this rug?"

"The boy who led me to your store. He brought it only two minutes ago, from the backroom where you had gone."

Kevork remained silent. He could distinctly remember having remained all the time alone in his storeroom. The American noted that Kevork seemed puzzled and added:

"You know, that tall dark boy with the slit eyes, the one in the odd costume who brought me to your store. I guess he works for you."

The American remained silent for a while, when he returned to his contemplation of the gold-threaded rug. Finally he exclaimed:

"It's beautiful. I'll take it. *Kaç para?* How much do you want for it?"

Kevork named his price, a stiff one. Without any hesitation, the American pulled out of his hip pocket a roll of his green paper money, calculated roughly how many dollars Kevork's price would mean, paid on the spot, picked up the rug and walked out of the shop, not even bothering to collect change on the round sum that he had just handed to the dealer. Three months later, Kevork received a letter from America, thanking him for the rug: "It hangs here on the wall of my room, where I can see it from my bed before I fall asleep and when I wake up. One night, I even dreamed about it and saw a beautiful girl weaving it. She wore a strange dress and looked very sad. Somehow, she reminded me very much of the photographs of my own Indian mother, whom I have never known because she died when I was born."

AN AILMENT THAT SPREAD FAST AND FAR

Accustomed as Mother Fatma became, with advancing age, to cope in her own way with a constant crescendo of misfortunes and ills, this particular market day seemed to be fraught with troubles that were almost more than she could bear. Her back had long been racked by pains that bent it until her head was bowed nearly to her knees. Her legs, for the last couple of years, had been so bruised and inflamed that she could barely walk. Malevolent neighbors appeared to encourage their children to steal from her tiny garden the fruit and vegetables that were her only livelihood. How she raised them was a mystery: she was never seen to work at all in her garden and had nobody to help her. It was even whispered that a familiar spirit must garden for her invisibly or at night.

For the past couple of weeks, one of the wheels of her little wooden pushcart now kept on falling loose, so that she would upset her small load of fruit and vegetables, in the mud of the alleys of old Stamboul, several times on her way to the market where she was barely able to sell them. The day before, she had trekked wearily across the whole city to ask her son to mend the wheel for her, but had been angrily greeted by her daughter-in-law, who forbade her ever to show her ungraceful person again in their neighborhood where all who saw her would suspect her, from her appearance, of being a witch. This very morning, Mother Fatma had found herself afflicted besides with a hemorrhoid of such proportions that every movement was sheer agony.

Still, she set forth, with her pushcart, to sell her few goods in the market. Never had it taken her so long to get there. Perhaps because she went so slowly and carefully, the loose wheel failed to fall off during the two hours of her trek. But when she reached the crowded market, a heavily loaded donkey backed into her cart, knocked the wheel off, and scattered all her fruit and vegetables in the mud. With infinite pain, she bent down again and again to gather up her goods, trying to save as much as she could from being trampled underfoot in the bustling crowd. All around her, pandemonium seemed to break loose as she held up traffic in the narrow lane between the crowded shops. One of the market police, a strapping young fellow with bellicose mustaches and a loud voice, soon descended upon her, urging her angrily to move on faster. Obstinate as old people often are, she continued to pick up her goods and hold up the traffic. The policeman, a certain Corporal Rashid, stood there insulting her, too proud of his uniform to help her in her predicament. Then he grabbed her by the arm and forced her to move on at his own brisk pace. Tortured by the pain inflicted on her by every one of her movements, Mother Fatma exclaimed:

"Young man, have you no respect for age and infirmities? If you had a hemorrhoid like mine, you too would no longer be able to walk so briskly."

Suddenly, the new pain that had stabbed her all morning vanished. She looked up, saw the young policeman wince and hobble off without uttering a word, obviously in great physical distress. She laughed, cackling like an evil old hen, and returned to her business.

Corporal Rashid managed only with great difficulty to limp

back, with bended knee to reduce his pain, from the market to the police station. There he was greeted in stentorian tones by his immediate superior, Sergeant Ali, who bawled him out for his slouching gait that would disgrace the police force in the eyes of the public: "Stand up straight, man! Quick, march!" Under his breath, Corporal Rashid mumbled: "I'd like to see you stand up straight and quick-march briskly if you had a hemorrhoid like mine."

Immediately, he felt immensely relieved, stood up straight, and was able to quick-march across the yard without further pain. Looking back, he saw Sergeant Ali wince and hobble off into his office, obviously in agony and cursing as he went.

Later that afternoon, Sergeant Ali was most distressed when a messenger came to summon him at once, on urgent business, to police headquarters. Slowly and with great pain, he managed to hobble the long way there, from his marketplace *karaköl,* or police station, on the outskirts of the Old City, to the center of town. He was greeted, on his arrival, with a reprimand for having been so slow in answering the summons. But he held his breath and said nothing.

The chiefs of all the city's police stations had been brought together to receive instructions, from a Captain of the Palace Guard, about precautionary measures that would be needed, in a few days, on the occasion of the Sultan's state appearance, in the streets of the city, on his annual pilgrimage from the Palace to the very farthest of the many great Imperial mosques. Usually, the Sultan's vast retinue, on such occasions, attracted a considerable crowd that required some policing. On this particular occasion, the great distance covered by the procession, which would take several hours to reach the Mirimah Mosque and as many to return to Dolmahbahche Palace, made extra precautions necessary. Sergeant Ali's *karaköl* happened to be quite close to the mosque, so that he and his men would be responsible for preventing the crowd from seeking to enter the mosque in too large numbers or from hampering the movements of the Sultan and his retinue. The instructions were now being given

14

to the chiefs of the various responsible police stations by Captain Sabahattin, chief of the Sultan's own personal corps of guards.

Sabahattin Bey, Captain of the Guards of the Sultan's Palace, would have been considered a remarkably handsome military man in any land or age. But he owed to his mother's Arab ancestry an additional personal vanity that made him seek to stress the beauty of nature's endowments with the aid of the cosmetician's art. He thus increased the curve of his otherwise slightly bushy eyebrows by plucking them; he added a smear of bister to his eyelids so as to stress the white of his finely set eyes; he was always heavily perfumed and impeccably manicured, and he wore Viennese corsets, beneath his uniform, to increase the perfection of his already strikingly athletic figure. His mysterious private life led to much surmise in court circles.

The wives of several foreign ambassadors were reported to have swooned to no avail at his feet at diplomatic gatherings. In his official duties, he was respected as a disciplinarian. Abstemious in his habits, he appeared to be somewhat puritanical, a more devout Moslem than most other Palace officials. He was thus known to disappear, every once in a while, for several days at a time, after which he would return to the Palace pale and exhausted; it was rumored that he spent these mysterious leaves from his duties in a *tekke* or monastery of the mystical *Bektashi* sect, though some went further and asserted that he was even an initiate among the Mevlevi whirling dervishes.

Sabahattin Bey's manner was more distant than haughty as he now gave his instructions to the assembled local police chiefs. When he had finished, he asked the chief who would be responsible for the immediate area around the mosque to step forward for special instructions. Poor Sergeant Ali shuffled forward and slouched rather than stood at attention. Sabahattin Bey's sensitive eyebrows expressed surprise at so oddly undisciplined a gait and manner. Still, he gave his special instructions, after which Sergeant Ali tried feebly to salute and about-turn as briskly as he should, but uttered a heart-rending moan and

15

limped off to join the group of other local police chiefs. Saba-hattin Bey then called him back: "You'll have to put on a smarter show than that, Sergeant, on the day the Sultan appears in your district. If you can't pull yourself together, man, we'll have to appoint another sergeant there in your stead."

Sergeant Ali didn't dare utter a word but thought: "I'd like to see that fine feathered cock of an officer put on a smarter show than I'm doing now, if he had a pain like mine!"

At once Sergeant Ali felt miraculously relieved, stood up straight, clicked his heels briskly, snapped to attention, saluted, about-turned with ease, and marched off, a perfect example of military deportment. But he just found time to see, before about-turning, Sabahattin Bey's eyebrows twitch as if in acute agony while his whole face became suddenly as pale as that of a corpse.

Sabahattin Bey's sense of duty and his self-respect would never allow him to reveal to these assembled police chiefs the extent of the agony he was now suffering. Stiff as a poker, he walked slowly out of the room, as if attending an official fu-neral, but still a brave and perfectly military figure. Outside, in the yard, he vaulted onto his horse that a groom had been hold-ing for him and rode back to the Palace like a hero undergoing extreme torture and still refusing to betray the names of his ac-complices in an attempted political murder. Only once he had reached the Palace and was crossing the yard on which he had his private apartment, close to the Sultan's, did he at last relax, his brow moist with cold sweat, and reveal in his gait the nature of his pain. It was then that Sabahattin Bey was unfortunate enough, in the doorway, to meet Ayvash, the Sultan's favorite.

The boy seemed that day to be even more exasperatingly per-verse than usual. Though Ayvash owed his present fortunes en-tirely to Sabahattin Bey, who had been foolish enough to bring him into the Palace as one of his own attendants, after which Ayvash soon managed to arouse the Sultan's interest too, the boy now liked to tease his former protector and would even taunt him archly for having yielded so willingly to the Sultan's demands and relinquished all claims on him.

16

"What's up, dear Sabahattin?" the boy now teased as he minced along by the Captain's side. "You're walking as if some man had been playing on you the kind of trick you used to enjoy playing on me! Or has my jealous friend suspected you of still loving me and condemned you to be impaled? Poor Sabahattin, I often think of you even now. I don't suppose I'll ever have another friend as handsome as you, though you can be a bit of a bore, at times, with all the nonsense you preach to a boy about having to learn this and that and about thinking more of his future. Well, my future's turned out all right, hasn't it, even if I never took the trouble to learn all that you said that I should. Sabahattin, dear, I'll never forget what you've done for me, you know, and if you ever need my help, I'll gladly put in a good word for you!"

Sabahattin Bey cursed the boy under his breath and wished that Ayvash could suffer the pain he was now feeling. It might at least put a stop to his infernal chatter. Immediately, Sabahattin Bey felt relieved and was surprised to hear the boy let out a piercing scream. Ayvash leaned feebly against the wall and moaned: "Fancy that impotent and fat old man still managing to hurt a boy! All the time I lived with you, Sabahattin, and you're as much of a man as any I'm ever likely to know, nothing like this ever happened to me!" Ayvash burst into tears and tottered off to his own apartment, where he threw himself on his bed and wept and moaned for the rest of the afternoon.

The Caliph of All the Faithful, toward the end of the day, began to feel bored with affairs of state, ready to relax and enjoy a few moments of hard-earned privacy. As he left his Viziers in the hall where he still had important business to discuss with them, he informed them that he would join them again in an hour. In a playful mood, he entered his favorite's room. The boy lay on the bed, his face buried in a pillow, apparently fast asleep. The Sultan approached him on tiptoe and gently pinched his left buttock. Ayvash uttered a piercing scream: "You careless old fool! You've ruined me now for life, and there'll be no more fun and games unless that Jew doctor of yours can straighten

17

things out for me! I bet he has had plenty of occasions to do that kind of job on you, and if I could only wish it onto you he might have to tinker you up for the umpteenth time tonight!"

Ayvash stopped upbraiding the Sultan and turned pale. Suddenly, no longer feeling any pain, he realized how rashly he had been speaking. Would the Sultan be offended and turn him out of the Palace immediately, stripping him of all his jewels and other treasures and casting him out on an unfriendly world? Or would the Sultan even give orders that he be enclosed in a barrel lined with spikes, as other discarded favorites had been in the past, after which the barrel would be allowed to roll down the rocky slopes of one of the hills above the Bosphorus until it reached the waterfront and finally bounced into the sea? Ayvash shuddered all the more when he watched the Sultan, with an expression of extreme anguish, totter out of the room, moaning as he went.

In great agony, the Sultan returned to the hall where the Viziers were still awaiting him. There, he sank very gently into a particularly well-upholstered thronelike chair that had already been his late father's favorite seat in the last years of his reign, when his aging and sick body was racked by all sorts of incurable pains.

The Caliph of All the Faithful trembled like a jelly as he began to writhe awkwardly in this magnificent throne. Heavy drops of perspiration appeared on his brow. In a curiously faint and shrill voice, he called his Chief Eunuch, who stood close by: "Suleyman, Suleyman, send immediately for Doctor Del Medigo!" Moaning profusely and leaning for support on the shoulders of the two strongest men of the Palace Guard, the Sultan then retired to his private apartments and waited there, on his huge bed, in sheer agony. Accustomed as he was to believing, in orgies of self-pity, that all his woes were unique, the Caliph of All the Faithful muttered to himself: "Allah has reserved for me a pain that transcends anything that has afflicted any of my millions of subjects!"

Del Medigo Pasha, private physician to the Sultan, came of an ancient Spanish Jewish family that had practiced the physician's

18

art, from generation to generation, for close on a thousand years. Until the Inquisition forced its distinguished members to seek refuge in the Ottoman Empire, many of them had taught at the Universities of Salerno, Salamanca, and Montpellier. One of them, Rabbi Isaac ben Alcalai, had even been a pupil of the great Rambam, Moses Maimonides, one of the world's greatest theologians and, at the same time, a physician whose treatise on the nature and the treatment of hemorrhoids remained, for centuries, a medical classic. Del Medigo Pasha's ancestor then distinguished himself by writing a commentary on the Rambam's treatise, enlarging mainly on sorcery as one of the possible causes of hemorrhoids and on the special treatments required when sorcery might be suspected as an etiological factor. Rabbi Isaac ben Alcalai Del Medigo thus described in considerable detail the symptoms of hemorrhoids caused by sorcery, their abnormal size, their very sudden appearance, their peculiarly greenish color and almost fungoid texture, etc. . . . He cited historical examples, including one quite legendary hemorrhoid with which one of the Companions of the Prophet was reported to have been afflicted in Mecca; it had been cured by a Jewish physician, one of the Black Jews of Abyssinia, who appeared in Mecca almost miraculously and was never seen again after performing this cure, which consisted in a light massage of the affected area, accompanied by an appropriate formula for exorcising evil spells, then followed by a treatment that relied mainly on the magic qualities of the letters of the Hebrew alphabet. Rabbi Isaac ben Alcalai Del Medigo found this curious legend in ancient Arabic chronicles where the Hebrew texts of the formula and of the subsequent treatment, a kind of poultice of herbs wrapped in linen inscribed with these Hebrew characters, had been somewhat badly garbled. Still, after many years of puzzling and of cabalistic study, the good Rabbi figured it all out. Then, one day, to his immense gratification, he was visited by one of those rare patients who happen, every once in a while, to be afflicted with the kind of hemorrhoid that leads a wary physician to suspect sorcery rather than a physical disorder as its cause. Rabbi Isaac ben Alcalai Del Medigo was overjoyed when

19

this opportunity to try out his formula arose. To his immense gratification, the therapy proved to be effective. He then consigned in his treatise, for the benefit of posterity, his rare knowledge.

Posterity was none too appreciative of the Rabbi's lore, especially in our own centuries of increasing enlightenment. In fact, only one manuscript copy of his treatise was known to have survived, in the Library of the University of Montpellier, where Rabbi Isaac ben Alcalai Del Medigo had once taught. Nor had any medical scholar or student of medieval Semitic literature ever deemed this manuscript worthy of a critical edition as a curiosity of medical literature. It remained there, in the University of Montpellier, without a single reader for a good two centuries, till a young Spanish Jewish student from Constantinople, a certain Nissim Del Medigo, unexpectedly turned up during the reign of King Louis-Philippe of France to obtain instruction in the empirical disciplines of modern medical science. The young man happened to be able to read Hebrew, and the Chief Librarian, an admirer of the great scholar Victor Cousin and himself an amateur medievalist of sorts, though with notions of the Middle Ages that reeked of Romanticism, one day asked Nissim Del Medigo to help him catalogue the University's collection of medieval Hebrew manuscripts. Nissim Del Medigo was much surprised to discover, among these long-forgotten tomes, the only known copy of his own ancestor's otherwise quite legendary work. He read it with great difficulty and some skepticism. Later, after obtaining his medical degree, he returned to his native Constantinople and made a great career as the Ottoman capital's leading physician, even becoming, within ten years, private physician to the Sultan, the very Caliph of All the Faithful.

Haunted by a curious piety, he decided, as soon as time and his own fortunes would allow it, to do something in order to rescue from oblivion his strange ancestor's treatise. Only recently, Del Medigo Pasha had therefore commissioned a specialist in the field of medieval Hebrew literature to copy the Montpellier manuscript at his expense and to prepare, for publication,

20

a critical edition of it which he himself, as a physician, would then preface with observations reflecting a medical point of view.

The Hebrew scholar's manuscript of this book had at long last arrived from France that very morning, and Del Medigo Pasha happened to be reading it, with some amusement, when a messenger arrived to summon him immediately to the Palace. Actually, he had just finished reading Rabbi Isaac ben Alcalai Del Medigo's careful description of the only hemorrhoid of magical etiology that he had ever been privileged to diagnose and to treat. The Rabbi explained that he refrained from operating on it as this would have been fatal to the patient. But he also refrained from advising the patient to wish it on another, as this would have been immoral, contrary to the ethics implied by the Hippocratic Oath. Because it had originally been inflicted on a sufferer as an after-effect of some bestial practices of sorcery, he had not hesitated, however, to inflict it again, through white magic, on the one who had started the chain of sufferers by meddling in black magic. By midnight of the same day, the Rabbi knew, this original sufferer, whoever he or she might be, would be afflicted again with the evil ailment and would immediately die of it.

Del Medigo Pasha was reading this passage of the manuscript when the messenger came to summon him in haste to the Palace. The physician could scarcely believe his eyes when he later diagnosed, on the body of the Caliph of All the Faithful, exactly the ailment that was described in his ancestor's treatise. Never, in any of the modern literature on hemorrhoids, had he seen such a huge one described, of so strange a color and texture. To operate upon it would pose great problems, especially as the Sultan could not be treated like any other mortal in a hospital or clinic. Del Medigo Pasha decided to try, for what it might be worth, his distinguished ancestor's treatments. To reduce the Sultan's pain temporarily, he applied, however, an anesthetizing ointment, which would allow him time to return to his home to fetch the manuscript, study it in detail, and procure the necessary ingredients for the magic poultice.

An hour and a half later, Del Medigo Pasha was back at the

Palace. He had procured the herbs for the poultice, written in his own hand the Hebrew text on clean linen, and was ready to try the effectiveness of this obsolete cure. The Sultan was still in great pain, though the anesthetizing ointment was having some slight effect. Del Medigo Pasha explained to his patient the kind of treatment that he now proposed to try.

"Whether you believe it or not, *Votre Altesse Impériale,* this ailment may be a curse that has been wished on you by someone who was already suffering from it and could be cured of it only by wishing it onto another potential sufferer. Of course, I could advise you to wish it at random on someone else, but it might be harmful to have such a disturbing ailment spreading from one of your subjects to the next, causing distress to as many as a dozen of them in a day. Fortunately, there is another cure, known only to me. To operate upon it, as any other physician might be tempted to do, would be immediately fatal to you. What I propose to do now, *Votre Altesse Impériale,* is to apply to your august person the same treatment as another physician of my race once applied to one of the Companions of the Prophet, who was afflicted with the same ill. If the magical treatment works, your ailment will suddenly vanish, destined to reappear immediately on the first person who suffered from it today. This unfortunate person, whoever he or she may be, will then die of it in the course of the night. *Votre Altesse Impériale* was indeed very fortunate to catch it so late in the day! Had you had it in the morning without my knowing, and cured yourself by wishing it onto another, and had I then been summoned at this hour to diagnose it on another patient, I might unwittingly, by applying this treatment, have sent it back to *Votre Altesse Impériale* and thus been the indirect cause of a national bereavement. As it is, I tremble to think of the unfortunate who must now die—it's already half past eight—within the next three and a half hours."

Del Medigo Pasha followed the prescription he had found in his distinguished ancestor's treatise. The Caliph of All the Faithful stood before him, perfectly naked and on all fours on his bed, as the Jewish physician applied his finger to the affected area and spread on it an ointment before applying the magic poultice too. Thanks to the ointment, the poultice clung to the affected area. The Sultan suddenly felt no more pain. The poultice dropped off, revealing that the ill had vanished.

Relieved but still weak from the pain that he had endured, the Sultan could only smile feebly as he teased his trusted physician: "These Jews, Del Medigo Pasha, they get their fingers in everywhere! But you're more than a doctor, you're a real magician!" The Captain of the Palace Guard, Sabahattin Bey, was then summoned and instructed by the Sultan to distribute toys and sweetmeats and comforts in all of Constantinople's Jewish orphanages, hospitals, and homes for the sick, the aged, and the destitute. On his return to his own apartment, he found a weeping Ayvash awaiting him. The Sultan had already told the boy that his services were no longer needed and that he must now fend for himself. But Sabahattin Bey was wise enough to know that he too would no longer need the services of so petulant and pert a former Imperial favorite. Ayvash was immediately packed off to a distant *tekke* of whirling dervishes in Anatolia, to serve there as a novice while being initiated into their rites and doctrines.

Late the next evening, Mother Fatma's neighbors began to worry. All day, the old woman had not been seen to emerge, as was her wont, from her hovel. During the preceding night they had heard her scream, but she often screamed in her sleep, and they now paid no more attention to the din than on other occasions. Still, they sent one of the children into the hovel to find out if she were there. The child returned somewhat awed: the old woman appeared to be lying dead in her miserable bedding. When the neighborhood hags washed the corpse for the funeral, they were horrified to find on it a monstrous hemorrhoid of a truly satanic texture and hue. They knew at once that this could have been produced only by sorcery, in fact by Mother Fatma's bestial intercourse with the evil *djinn* who had long been her familiar spirit, her gardener, and her lover.

THE GHOST POPO

An inordinate passion for all the fads and fashions of the Western world has long been one of the weaknesses of our aristocrats, few of whom remain content with the traditional customs and ways of our own civilization. Some decades ago, it thus came to pass that a certain Murad Bey, who had spent many years as a diplomat in our embassies in foreign capitals, retired in his old age to a magnificent *yali,* or waterfront villa, on the Bosphorus, where he proceded to dazzle his more intimate friends by entertaining them in a manner which revealed his knowledge of the life of such exotic capitals as Paris, Vienna, and Munich. Among other luxuries, he had brought back from Munich, where he had spent many years, a gallery of oil paintings which had much in common with the collection that a Bavarian King once made by ordering portraits of all the great beauties of his court. Murad Bey's collection, however, instead of revealing the facial features of the European ladies who had been his mistresses, displayed only their buttocks. One could thus admire, in his gallery of beauties, realistic portraits of the

Popo of La Paiva and of other famous courtesans of the Western world, and Murad Bey would explain his choice of this particular aspect of his mistresses, for the portraits which he commissioned, by insisting that the ladies concerned owed their fortunes to those charms with which Allah endowed them from the waist downward rather than to those others which, like the much less important visible part of an iceberg appearing above the waters, were more generally revealed to the public, as is the custom in Western lands, where even the most virtuous women parade the streets barefaced.

There were thirty-five such portraits in Murad Bey's gallery, which he proudly exhibited only to his closest friends, but where he also spent much of his spare time meditating his own glorious past as a diplomat and *bon vivant* in the great capitals of Europe.

One day, as Murad Bey took his morning coffee in solitary state, as was his custom, in his Gallery of Beauties, he was suddenly surprised to see a thirty-sixth Popo exhibited on its walls, in fact in a place of honor, in the panel above the fireplace where, until now, there had always been a somewhat less personal souvenir of his years spent abroad, in fact a flowerpiece of the Dutch school. This new Popo was moreover of quite remarkable beauty and, at the same time, awakened no memories at all in Murad Bey's mind, only a burning desire of a kind that he was no longer accustomed to feel.

Murad Bey approached the mysterious portrait and began to examine it more carefully. It was exactly of the same size as the Dutch flowerpiece, in fact hanging there, so it seemed, in the same carved and gilded antique frame. Apprehensive of making a fool of himself as the victim of some practical joke, Murad Bey decided, for the time being, not to inquire into the origins of the mysterious new Popo, but to watch carefully the reactions of his retainers so as to find out whether any of them had been an accomplice in this trick that he suspected one of his friends of having played on him. Half an hour later, the majordomo who always brought Murad Bey his coffee entered the room

25

again to remove the tray with the empty cup; though he stood a good five minutes facing the mysterious portrait while Murad Bey gave him various orders for the day, the man's face revealed absolutely no awareness of any change in the decoration of the room. He indeed stood there as if he were facing but the Dutch flowerpiece that had been hanging above the fireplace for many years. Murad Bey was even more mystified, and subsequently spent most of the day in his private gallery, watching the reactions of all who came and went. Not one of his servants revealed, in the course of that otherwise uneventful day, any awareness of change in the appointments of the room.

Late that afternoon, Murad Bey received the visit of one of his boon companions, a retired diplomat like himself, Reshat Bey, who had spent many years with him in the Turkish embassy in Munich and even advised him, at times, in the choice of the painters whom he should commission for these portraits, being more of a connoisseur of art than of the natural beauties which can inspire an artist. As they drank coffee together in the gallery and spoke of old times, Reshat Bey examined all the portraits, as he always did, reminded by each in turn of some adventure of their common past in Western Europe, but paid no attention at all to the mysterious new Popo, passing in front of it exactly as if the Dutch flowerpiece which had always hung there were still in evidence in its frame. Murad Bey was more mystified than ever when Reshat Bey even pointed out to him that the petals of one of the tulips in the flowerpiece would soon need the attentions of a good restorer. Apparently, Reshat Bey could still see there but the usual masterpiece of Dutch art.

The next morning, when Murad Bey awoke somewhat earlier than usual and ordered his majordomo to serve him his coffee in the gallery, he was even more surprised to see that it now exhibited, as usual, only thirty-five portraits and the Dutch flowerpiece which had appeared to be missing the previous day but that Reshat Bey had still been able to see. Again, all day, nothing in the behavior of Murad's servants could reveal an awareness of anything at all unusual. For several months, this state

26

of affairs continued: sometimes the thirty-sixth Popo was hanging above the fireplace in the gallery, apparently visible only to Murad Bey, though sometimes too he would see there only the Dutch flowerpiece. Nor did there seem to be any particular reason for the somewhat capricious private appearances of the thirty-sixth Popo. It just came and went according to its own sweet whims, its comings and goings having no relationship at all to any moods or events in poor Murad Bey's life. Gradually, Murad Bey began to suffer from insomnia. In the middle of the night, he would wake up suddenly, wondering whether he would find the mysterious Popo or the Dutch flowerpiece hanging in his gallery. Tiptoeing from his room so as not to arouse the suspicions of his own household, he would enter the gallery to see what he would find there. He even developed an interest in statistics, mathematics, and probability calculations, often betting in secret on the probable appearance of the Popo or of the Dutch flowerpiece. If he lost his bet, which usually happened, he would dutifully, being a man of honor, pay the sum he had lost to a religious foundation the very next day, generally to a home for the widows of soldiers killed in our disastrous Caucasian campaigns against the Tsar. Gradually, Murad Bey thus acquired a considerable reputation as a philanthropist.

Now it came to pass, about a year later, that Reshat Bey, on the occasion of one of the numerous visits to his old friend and colleague in the course of which they discussed the past and drank coffee together in the gallery, chanced to mention, one afternoon, a piece of gossip that had recently spread throughout the capital from the infamous cafés that sailors and other common people frequent along the waterfront in Karaköy and Tophane. According to this rumor, a café in Tophane had engaged a new dancer, a Greek from Asia Minor, whose extraordinarily beautiful Popo already inspired love songs which immediately became popular and were sung throughout the city. The point of the story was, however, that this dancer of the popular *tsivtiteli* of the mountain villages behind Smyrna, reputed now to be endowed with the most beautiful Popo in the whole of the Ottoman

27

Empire, was not a girl but a boy. Murad Bey, known internationally as an expert in the field of the beauty of the female Popo, hotly contested this rumor, which he dismissed as sheer nonsense, a sign of the decadence of the times and a proof of the unfortunate spread of pederasty in the working classes, perhaps as a consequence of the massive migration of unmarried men from the villages of Arab Syria, all of them seeking work in the overcrowded capital. However common in Arab countries, such vices were indeed, in Murad Bey's opinion, utterly alien to the Turkish way of life.

Though neither Murad Bey nor Reshat Bey had ever been known to be at all interested in the Popo of a boy, the discussion was hot. Murad Bey was adamant in denying any possible truth in the rumor that Reshat Bey reported; Reshat Bey, on the other hand, argued that there cannot be smoke without some fire and that a popular rumor which was already so widespread must surely be founded on some fact. Finally, they decided to go that very evening to investigate the matter themselves. Reshat Bey's carriage and coachman were still waiting outside Murad Bey's *yali,* to drive him back, after his afternoon visit, to the capital, where he lived in a luxurious *garçonnière* that overlooked the Golden Horn, on the heights of Tepebahce, near the Pera Palace Hotel. So they drove together into the city, dined comfortably at Abdallah's world-famous restaurant, then proceeded downtown to the more disreputable quarters of Karaköy and Tophane.

The café that they were seeking was not difficult to find: the first sailor from whom their coachman inquired was able to instruct them how to reach it. It proved to be a fairly large establishment, somewhat cleaner and more decent than they expected, crowded with men from every walk of life, but with a majority of sailors and of none too reliable waterfront types. At the back of the hall there was a small stage, which was empty as they entered the room. The Armenian proprietor of the café, sensing that he had to deal with guests of some distinction, led Murad Bey and Reshat Bey to a kind of table of honor, set apart from the crowd but at the same time situated in such a way that they had an excellent view of the stage. Feeling themselves obliged to put on some show of largesse, Murad Bey and Reshat Bey ordered champagne, fully expecting to be served a ghastly concoction concealed in the discarded French bottle of a more reputable establishment; a few minutes later, they were delighted to find that they were being served an excellent Geissler Frères of an unusually good vintage year, quite properly iced.

Murad Bey was gratified when he was able to point out, in support of his theory concerning the alien nature, in Turkey, of such abnormal passions as Reshat Bey reported to him to be now current in the capital, the presence, in the crowd, of a large number of obviously Arab officers of the Sultan's armed forces, who even dared appear here in uniform. *"Triste époque!"* he sighed, in perfect French.

After a while, when the hall was crowded, the entertainment began, at first with an Anatolian folk singer who played his *saz* and sang popular ballads which were much applauded. Then there appeared on the stage a creature of superlative but strange beauty, more feminine than any woman that Murad Bey or Reshat Bey had ever seen, and whose every movement was like an amiable parody of those of a woman or like a sublime imitation of them. As this creature danced, its hips, arms, and shoulders moved with such grace and sensuality that every man in the hall was enraptured. The Arab officers were quite shameless in their applause, and a shower of silver and gold coins soon began to fall on the stage, all around the dancer on whose brow, at one point, a glass of water was placed, while the creature continued to perform with its back to the audience, slowly bending back until its head touched the floor, without ever spilling the water from the glass. This rare trick was greeted with delirious applause. During the applause, the creature suddenly lowered its silken Turkish trousers, such as women wear, and revealed a pair of ravishing buttocks that were quivering to the same rhythm as its shoulders; at the same time it also bared its breasts, stripping them of their artificial padding, and then

29

turned briskly to reveal to the audience its real nature, that of a boy.

For a few seconds, Murad Bey had been able to recognize the original of the mysterious thirty-sixth Popo of his private gallery of portraits. He was so shocked that he swooned. Reshat Bey, who knew none of the circumstances of this strange recognition scene, as dramatic as that of *Iphigenia in Tauris,* attributed his friend's emotion, with some surprise, to the effects of love at first sight. But he called immediately for a physician, who prescribed the application of leeches and several days' rest, which Murad Bey spent in his friend's *garçonnière* in the city, so as to be closer to his physician, should the need for further treatments arise.

During these days of convalescence, Murad Bey was strangely silent, and his friend, a man of real tact, was careful to avoid any allusion to the occasion of the patient's sudden collapse. On the third day, however, Murad Bey could stand his perplexity no longer and opened his heart to his friend, who could scarcely believe his ears. Together, they then drove to Murad Bey's *yali* on the shore of the Bosphorus. There, in the gallery, they both inspected the delinquent Dutch flowerpiece, which hung there as it had for many years. Reshat Bey began to suspect his old friend of suffering from hallucinations and tactfully commented on certain recent and disturbing rumors of impending war as they both sat and drank coffee, with their backs to the flowerpiece, enjoying the view of the Bosphorus through the gallery's window. Suddenly, Reshat Bey turned to see what time it might be by the mantlepiece clock. He gasped: the flowerpiece, while they had been sitting with their backs to it, had truly changed into a portrait of a thirty-sixth Popo which Reshat Bey immediately recognized as the one they had seen together, a few nights earlier, in the café in Tophane. Hearing his friend gasp, Murad Bey turned around too, saw the thirty-sixth Popo and fainted again.

A few days later, the two friends decided to investigate this whole mysterious business together. First, they returned to the

30

café in Tophane, to question the boy-dancer. Much to their surprise, the boy, a certain Spiridion Stavropoulos, seemed to be well-acquainted with Murad Bey's gallery of portraits of great European beauties. Questioned in greater detail, it turned out that Spiridion, one summer night when Murad Bey was away from Istanbul, taking the waters at Bursa, had been brought back to the *yali* on the shores of the Bosphorus by Murad Bey's coachman, an Albanian who, like many men of his race, was passionately addicted to the smoking of hashish and to pederasty. There, the coachman took the liberty of showing the boy some of the treasures of the aristocratic home where he was spending the night, including the famous gallery of portraits of European beauties. Immediately, Spiridion had become possessed with the monstrous and absurd ambition of some day seeing his own portrait added to the distinguished collection. Some months later, having failed ever to meet the somewhat misanthropically retired owner of the *yali* and thus have this portrait commissioned as an addition to the gallery, Spiridion consulted an Anatolian sorceress who prepared for him a love-filter which Spiridion asked the coachman to hang, in the gallery, at the back of the only painting there that did not represent a Popo, that is to say the Dutch flowerpiece. From that day on, the apparitions of the mysterious thirty-sixth Popo had begun to take place, but visible only to connoisseurs of this particular part of the human anatomy, that is to say to the coachman, who rarely entered the gallery, to Murad Bey, and finally, after their visit to Tophane, to Reshat Bey, who had now become a belated convert to this cult.

Charmed by the boy's confession, Murad Bey could only grant his wish. The famous Paris painter Henner was summoned to Istanbul on the spot, to paint the boy's portrait as he had already painted those of other famous beauties. After that, Murad Bey's gallery always exhibited thirty-six portraits, the Dutch flowerpiece having now been relegated to the coachman's room, where it continued, every once in a while, to appear as a replica of the Henner masterpiece that was hanging in the gallery.

31

THE BOULISSA'S PILGRIMAGE

The octogenarian Boulissa de Tazartis was the dowager of the powerful Romaniot-Jewish Tazartis family, bankers for several generations to His Imperial Highness the Sultan *"de toutes les Turquies,"* as the old lady's more Westernized grandson, Kalonymos (Shemtov) Tazartis, would say in his irreverent Parisian manner. For many years, she had now lived quietly in her huge frame *konak,* a palace built on a hill in Hasköy above the shore of the Golden Horn. Suddenly, one morning, within five minutes of her awakening, the whole house was in an uproar destined to last all day and several days to come.

When her maid, a Polish girl from the village of Polonesköy on the Asiatic shore of the Bosphorus, brought to the Boulissa that morning her daily cup of steaming Turkish coffee, the old lady had calmly announced: "I'm going to Jerusalem on a pilgrimage. I dreamed last night that I was dying there. That kind of dream always comes true."

She was known as the Boulissa throughout the city, as if her name, meaning "counsellor" in her Romaniot Greek dialect,

32

were an official title. Her age could be estimated only on the basis of the reckonings of her increasingly rare contemporaries who, in a land where births were not yet officially registered, were the only reliable sources of information in such matters. For the past ten years the Boulissa had not moved from Constantinople, not even to spend the hot summer months on the island of Prinkipo, in the Sea of Marmara, or in one of the seaside resorts of the Bosphorus where it had long been her custom to go every year. The announcement of her intended pilgrimage therefore caused almost as much consternation as might that of her sudden death. Her whole household agreed, though without mentioning it so as to avoid attracting the attention of the Evil Eye, that the Boulissa would never survive the strain of such a long trip. From her own utterances, it was clear, besides, that she had no intention of returning to Constantinople, should she ever reach Jerusalem alive.

Spanish, French, Greek, and Turkish predominated in the hubbub of voices that lamented and commented on her decision, while smaller groups could be found, in odd corners of the rambling wooden palace, discussing the disaster in other languages of the far-flung Ottoman Empire, in Armenian or Kurdish, in Arabic or Albanian. As the day advanced and the news began to spread throughout the city, the crowds that converged on the house and the uproar within its walls became almost threatening. Ever since her marriage, over sixty years ago, the Boulissa, who had borne her first son when she was only seventeen, had lived in this old *konak,* refusing to move from it when her husband died and the whole neighborhood later began to deteriorate. By now, it was the only great household left in Hasköy, all other wealthier Jewish families having moved to more fashionable neighborhoods. The Boulissa's manifold charities were known, moreover, throughout the city. On the eve of every Sabbath, for instance, an hour before the Holy Day began, she appeared each week on her balcony above the narrow street, to distribute to the poor of every creed whatever small change, *bozuk para* or "broken money," remained in her purse from her whole week's spending allowance. As the crowds that awaited her weekly largesse grew through the years, the Boulissa's sons and grandsons began to supplement her small change with bags of coppers that a messenger brought to her home each Friday morning from the offices of their bank.

The *Haham,* or Grand Rabbi, and a whole flock of other rabbis visited the Boulissa regularly, to consult her on the community's welfare problems. Greek Orthodox "popes," Armenian priests, the Catholic clergy of the Levantines of Galata and Pera, even Moslem mullahs and dervishes from a neighboring *tekke* or religious foundation, came likewise to pay their respects to her and thank her for her kindnesses to their coreligionaries. One such visitor, a holy man of some unidentified religion, was reputed to be a priest of the mysterious Yazid fireworshippers, the Zoroastrians of the eastern Anatolian mountains. Or was he a Hindu fakir? His fits and prophetic utterances were too frightening to be those of a charlatan. The *konak* itself, as the years went by, had become moreover a refuge for unfortunates of every kind and creed, ranging from the widowed mother of a former Albanian coachman who had been knifed in a drunken brawl to three unmarried nieces of the Boulissa who had fled penniless to Constantinople, during one of the Balkan Wars, from a Bulgarian city where the conquered Turks and their loyal Jewish agents were being massacred by the victorious Christians. By now, nobody knew exactly how many such unfortunates lived in the Boulissa's home. In neighboring hovels, numerous other dependents of one sort or another had also settled, subsisting on crumbs from her lavish table and on her own direct bounties. She was reputed never to wear a new petticoat more than a day: within twenty-four hours, she would always find some worthy recipient who, she felt, needed it more than she.

The Boulissa's imminent departure for Jerusalem and the possibility of her dying there and never returning to Constantinople spelled disaster for scores of her dependents, without counting all those who lived mainly on her charities in the welfare institutions of the community. But the Boulissa was adamant in her decision, even when the *Haham* called to argue with her. "For the good of my soul," she declared, "I have done all that I can here. I must see the Holy City before I die." In any case, she would make ample provision for her household and her charities before abandoning the Imperial City. Nor did she feel that she was destined to live much longer, even were she to remain in Constantinople. After her death, her sons and grandsons, she hoped, would carry on the traditions of her good works; but this no longer depended on her own decisions.

As the days went by, great progress was made with preparations for her departure. The huge house was stripped of its precious carpets, its silverware and Dresden china; the Boulissa was distributing all unnecessary luxuries as souvenirs to her family and friends. Huge stores of useful clothing and of non-perishable foodstuffs were delivered to the house in their stead, to provide for the needs of its remaining dependents. Messengers were sent to warn the notables of Jewish communities between Constantinople and Jerusalem that they were to prepare for the Boulissa's arrival, wherever her ship was expected to stop, in Smyrna, for instance, in Iskenderun and in Beyrouth, as well as in some inland cities, such as Aleppo, where she had relatives, friends, or charities that she could not afford to neglect. Her own baggage, for the trip, was considerable, though in no way extravagant: it seemed to consist mainly of gifts which she intended to distribute on her way. But the number of her travel companions increased as the days went by, either because her piety inspired other members of the community to accompany her on her pilgrimage, or else because so many people preferred not to face the risks of no longer being able to live on her bounties or in her immediate presence. Finally, her train consisted of fifty-two people, including two Moslems and five Christians of various denominations. At the last minute, the Boulissa's old friend, the Sultana Walideh, or dowager mother of the Sultan, even persuaded her son to send an armed guard of ten men, captained by a *shaoush*, or sergeant, to protect the pilgrims on their journey and thus give the whole venture an almost official character.

As the Boulissa and her traveling companions boarded their ship on the landing stage in Galata, the turmoil was quite unprecedented, the news of her sailing having meanwhile spread throughout the city and attracted hundreds of curious idlers in addition to her own many relatives, friends, and well-wishers. That morning, Hajji Bekir, the city's world-famous confectioner, did as much business as on a *Sheker Bayram,* the annual Moslem feast when the faithful offer sweetmeats to all their friends. Hundreds of people came to purchase parcels of *rahat loukoum* to bring as a parting gift to the Boulissa. She and her train might well have subsisted on Turkish delight alone, all the way from Constantinople to Jerusalem. But the Boulissa refused to accept gifts and ordered that they be immediately distributed to local hospitals and homes for orphans or old people.

The turmoil on the landing stage reached its peak when the Sultana Walideh in person arrived, heavily veiled as she emerged from the closed carriage in which she had come with her usual official retinue of armed guards and eunuchs. In the privacy of the Boulissa's cabin, the mother of the reigning Sultan raised her veil briefly to kiss her old friend tenderly on the brow and on both cheeks. As an afterthought, she muttered a prayer in Arabic and kissed her again on both eyes, her trembling lips pausing on each eye for a long while. The two women wept silently, then parted. They knew that they would never meet again, as they had done regularly for many years, to discuss together the problems of the city's numerous indigents. But the Sultana's armed guard remained aboard the ship. The crowd on the landing stage appreciated the significance of this, and a murmur of approval was heard as the Sultana departed with only her usual retinue of enunuchs. When her hand appeared at the curtained window of her carriage in a modest gesture of greeting, an ovation arose, interspersed with enthusiastic whistling and keening.

The *Haham* brought the Boulissa, among other gifts, one that she deigned to accept: a pillow of velvet that contained earth from the Holy Land, for her to rest her head, should the Angel of Death call for her before she reached her distant destination. The pillow was moreover embroidered, in heavy gold thread, with 'a prayer in Hebrew, wishing her the fulfillment of all her prayers, like a kind of blank check on the graciousness of God; besides, at its four corners, the pillow was adorned with tassels of blue turquoise beads to ward off the Evil Eye. Finally, to the prow of the ship, the *Haham* attached another amulet of blue beads to protect it and its passengers against storms at sea and all other wiles of the Evil Eye that might assail the travelers; this amulet was a gift to the Boulissa from a saintly blind Moslem mullah who had been unable to attend her departure in person, being confined to his *tekke* by his infirmities.

One unfortunate incident marred the otherwise solemn scene, when the crowd on the pier suddenly parted to make way for Nissimaki Azizullah, the terror and disgrace of the Jewish "Nation" in the Ottoman capital, a drunken beggar of obscure Kurdish-Jewish, Daghestani, or Persian origin who had once been a pimp and now, blinded by a knife wound in one of his many waterfront brawls, still managed to subsist on the unwilling charities of the rich whom he insulted when their carriages rolled by his usual stand at the Galata end of the bridge that crosses the Golden Horn. Nissimaki employed for this purpose a depraved Armenian beggarboy who would point out to him the approaching carriages and reveal the names of their occupants. Accompanied by his effeminate companion, whose hips seemed to perform a *tsivtiteli* dance as he indecently minced rather than walked, Nissimaki now came to the foot of the gangway, called the Boulissa rudely forth, greeted her derisively as the *Sultana de los Desmazalados,* the Queen of the Ill-starred, poured a torrent of obscenities and threats on her innocent head in the presence of the shocked and silent crowd, then added an astounding prediction: "You'll be back in Stamboul before sunrise, you old fraud! You're too rich to see the Holy Land!" Without adding a word of explanation, Nissimaki

37

turned his back on the Boulissa, made his way through the threatening crowd and vanished.

An hour later, the ship sailed out of the Golden Horn, round the cape where stands the Sultan's Palace and into the Sea of Marmara, all its passengers assembled at the stern to cast a last nostalgic glance on the skyline of their beloved city and on its divinely beautiful strait of the Bosphorus where the continents of Asia and Europe so timidly refrain from joining in a true lovers' kiss. From one of the windows of the Imperial Palace, a blue silk scarf was waved in the wind to ward off the Evil Eye, a last greeting from the Sultana to her friend whom she respected as the true Queen of the *Millet* or "Nation" of the Jews of the Ottoman Empire. Later, as the ship passed the Islands of the Princes where the Boulissa had spent, in her childhood and girlhood, so many happy summer days, the Boulissa retired to her cabin for a meditative siesta.

She reappeared on the deck late in the afternoon, as the ship was about to pass the Island of Imrali. To the whole crew's astonishment, she now ordered that the ship turn back at once. She had just had another dream: Jerusalem was coming to her, so that she would now be able to die in a holy setting though still in her own home.

When she returned, with her whole train, late that night, to her abandoned *konak* in Hasköy, she found a saintly rabbi from Jerusalem awaiting her there. Quite independently, he had set forth, some months ago, to bring to the great lady the blessings of a community of Hassidim who had been able to pray in peace, thanks to her bounties, for many decades in the Holy City or in their mountainous retreat in Safed. The oldest and most saintly member of this community had recently been vouchsafed a dream in which he had been warned of the Boulissa's approaching death, after which he had sent one of the less frail brethren to bring her their greetings and prayers, since it no longer seemed likely that she would ever be able to visit them in the Holy Land as she had been planning to do for many years. The pilgrim had arrived at the *konak* a few hours after the Boulissa's departure, but had expressed no dismay when told that she had set forth on her trip. He only replied, quite confidently, that he would await there her return.

The Boulissa spent most of her time in the next few days in prayer with the saintly Hassid. One morning, about a week after her return, her Polish maid entered her room as usual to awaken her with her morning coffee, but found the Boulissa peacefully lying in her bed, the embroidered velvet pillow, given her by the *Haham,* placed beneath her head. She had died during the night.

THE IMPRISONED PRINCESS

A tale may be true even if no man can remember when it occurred or who were its protagonists. However mysterious and distant its origins, a legend may yet be a true story, remembered from generation to generation, blurred with age but enriched every once in a while with new trappings that revive its faded colors and perfume, like those of a garment once worn by a beautiful Princess, long dead, whose very name has been forgotten. Such a true story is the one that I am about to relate, about a Princess who was kept a prisoner in a lonely tower on a rock off the shores of the Bosphorus.

Was she a Turkish Princess or a daughter of one of the Greek Emperors of Byzantium? Today, none knows who she was, but the story of her misfortunes is true and the tower that had once been her prison still stands, though even archaeologists cannot agree about its origins. For at least five hundred years, perhaps for a thousand years or more, it has stood there, never known by any other name but the Tower of the Princess. If you examine its masonry, you will find that it was rebuilt about two hundred years ago as a lighthouse; that it had been fortified, about five hundred years ago, as an Ottoman watchtower; that it seems to have been, at some earlier date, a Genoese arsenal, perhaps even earlier a fortified landing stage for Amalfitan traders. Earlier still, it had been used by the Imperial Byzantine army as a link in its network of semaphores from which information and orders were signaled to and from the capital and throughout the Empire. Be that all as it may, the foundations of the tower, as it now stands, rest on the prostrate columns of a Greek temple that must have been demolished during the reign of one of the first Christian Emperors.

When did the Princess whose fate concerns us actually live imprisoned in this tower? No man can tell, and she has left no testimony of her misfortunes scrawled on the walls that remain. Perhaps she could neither read nor write; perhaps the wall on which she carved her complaint was sacrificed in the course of the tower's many subsequent structural changes. Still, it remains the Tower of the Princess, and I feel that it is my duty to recount the tale of her woes as it was once told to me.

"It was many and many a year ago, in a Kingdom by the Sea," and the ruler of that Kingdom that was all coasts and no hinterland, with the sea dividing even his capital, one part of the city being built on one continent and some of its suburbs across the narrow sea on the shores of another continent, was often hard put to it to keep the rulers of neighboring kingdoms at bay. For these other landlocked monarchs all coveted some access to the sea, and the Kingdom that was all coasts stood in their way, its integrity guaranteed mainly by treaties signed on the occasion of judiciously negotiated royal marriages whereby the King of the Coasts became the father-in-law of one of his more dangerous royal neighbors. The Princesses of this coastal Kingdom came in time to be valuable political assets. It was their duty to employ their physical and intellectual charms to reduce their royal mates to a less bellicose attitude and thus ensure the integrity of the frontiers of the coastal Kingdom.

Now it came to pass that one of these neighboring kingdoms,

41

as a consequence of such marriages, had been for many generations almost a vassal state of the Kingdom by the Sea, and was suddenly invaded by a wandering horde of ruthless Mongol barbarians. Unable to defend his territories, the defeated ruler fled to the capital of the Kingdom by the Sea, accompanied by his mother and his wife, both native Princesses of the capital city. Soon, the new ruler of the conquered inland Kingdom demanded threateningly some access to the sea. The Ruler of the Kingdom by the Sea then hastily consulted his aunt and his sister, the Queen Mother and the deposed Queen, who had fled to his court. They agreed, for reasons of state, to murder the refugee King and to offer his widow in marriage to the usurper, thereby granting him some kind of title to the throne that he occupied.

That very night, the foolish former ruler of the inland Kingdom was rudely awakened from his sleep, blinded, castrated, impaled, then cast from a tower to become a shapeless mess of torn flesh and fractured bones on the rocks of the seashore. As usual, it was announced to the populace that the unfortunate monarch had long been addicted to somnambulism.

After a barely decent period of mourning, an embassy was sent to the usurper, the widow accompanying it with a suitable retinue. But the uncouth conqueror of the Inland Kingdom took one look at her, sniffed haughtily and remarked that he had no use for a second-hand wife who also stank of carrion. Threatening war, he dismissed the whole embassy somewhat rudely. Ministers, courtiers, and Princesses returned helter-skelter to the capital by the sea, in undignified haste.

The Ruler of the Kingdom by the Sea then held a last desperate council of his ministers, at the outcome of which it was decided that the Empire's last remaining dynastic asset be sacrificed, a pampered Princess of fifteen years of age whose remarkable beauty should have earned her a less horrifying husband than this hairy usurper whose coarse hands were more accustomed to flattering the sweaty flanks of his battle-steed than to caressing the breasts of a carefully nurtured Princess of ancient lineage.

42

This time, the usurper was invited to come to the capital by the sea. Great festivities were organized in his honor. In the course of a banquet, the young Princess, decently draped in transparent veils that allowed one to imagine all her charms, was briefly produced in the gilded hall. The guest of honor smacked his lips coarsely as he saw her, but the Princess uttered a hysterical yell and had to be rushed back to her private quarters, where a flock of physicians applied leeches to her and bathed her again and again in warm infusions of borage and hyssop for the next few hours.

When she recovered from her access, she announced firmly that she refused, come what may, to marry such a monster. Only two things could now be done to save the situation. First, it was necessary to murder the visiting usurper: that very night, when he retired in a drunken stupor to rest, he was bitten by an asp concealed beneath his pillow. The next morning, when his corpse was found, it was explained that the asp must have found its way into the Palace in the visitor's baggage, such serpents being rare in the Kingdom by the Sea but common in the inland Kingdom.

But a second action remained necessary: to punish the Princess whose lack of patriotism might indeed have caused the ruin of her father's Kingdom. It was therefore announced that, heartbroken after the death of her betrothed, she had decided to withdraw for the rest of her days into a tower that rose from the rocks on the shore of the sea. That very day, the child-Princess was led from the Palace to this tower, where she spent the next few months in loneliness and desperation.

But the murdered usurper, though childless at his death, had two nephews, sons by his deceased brother's marriage to a kidnapped Persian Princess. The elder one of these nephews inherited the throne and soon became addicted to a life of debauchery that precluded the pursuit of any political or territorial ambitions such as those that his uncle had nourished. In no time, the court of the inland Kingdom became notoriously corrupt, the monarch himself, in the course of one of his orgies, becoming infected with a dread disease that was known to threaten both his reason and his life. Terrified of dying in his prime, the usurper's heir then became tyrannically suspicious of all who surrounded him, especially those who might presume to inherit his throne. Warned in good time, his younger brother escaped abroad and none knew where he had sought refuge. Younger princelings, all cousins, were disemboweled in short shrift in their baby-cots, their rotting heads then exhibited for weeks, on pikes, at the Palace gates.

When our Princess had already spent a good two years as a prisoner in her tower, she was kept awake, one night, by a raging storm. As the wind howled past her tower and the waves crashed on the rocks below, she suddenly seemed to hear a human cry. Rushing to her window, she discovered, in a flash of lightning, on the rocks beneath her balcony, an incredibly beautiful young man, presumably a fisherman whose fragile craft lay shattered among the rocks. He was drenched, almost naked, bleeding profusely from a wound in his side. Deeply moved, the Princess awakened her nurse, a devoted retainer who had accompanied her in her exile. Together, they then devised a plan to save the shipwrecked fisherman's life. They knew that their pitiless guards would rather let the young man die there on the rocks than allow him, however mortally wounded, into their tower. Weaving a ladder out of their knotted sheets and clothes, they climbed together, at the peril of their lives, from the balcony to the rocks below. Together, they then helped the wounded man up the ladder into their apartments and concealed him for the next few weeks, nursing him and sharing their food with him till he was well.

During these weeks, the wounded fisherman admitted, incredible though this may seem, that he was the fugitive heir apparent to the inland Kingdom. The Princess, in a fine romantic frenzy at the idea of falling in love with a poor fisherman, flatly refused to believe him. But when he had recovered, he vanished, one calm night, as mysteriously as he had appeared during a storm. For weeks, the Princess remained brokenhearted, listlessly playing cards all day or consulting the future in the grounds of innumerable cups of coffee.

44

Meanwhile, the debauched heir to the usurper slowly began to succumb to the illness that devoured his mind and his flesh. Stinking like a charnel house, he raved all day, none of his courtiers daring to approach him. Finally, alone one night in a drunken frenzy, he staggered to a vat of wine in the royal cellars, lost his balance, fell into the red liquid and was drowned. News of his ridiculous death soon spread far and wide, and his younger brother was able to return from abroad to be crowned King.

Immediately, the young King threatened to invade the Kingdom by the Sea, unless he be allowed to marry the imprisoned Princess. Terrified of his daughter's caprices, her father scarcely dared expect a successful outcome of this new royal visit and promptly ordered his chief minister to procure, as a precaution, another asp.

When the embassy from the inland Kingdom arrived in great pomp, the festivities began. Again, a great banquet was held. The visiting monarch shocked everyone by appearing there half-naked, in wet and torn clothes, like a shipwrecked sailor; a skillful cosmetician had even adorned his left side with an artificial wound from which the blood seemed to pour. In his horror, the royal host shifted uneasily on his throne, unconsciously pushing the lid off the golden box where the asp lay.

At last, the Princess appeared. As she saw the visiting monarch, she rushed toward him and swooned in his arms. At that moment, her father uttered a ghastly cry: the asp had bitten his left buttock. He died within an hour. After a decent delay, the marriage of the young King and of the Princess was celebrated, and the two Kingdoms thus became united, liberated from the threats of war which had cursed their relations in the past.

II

THE CHRONICLES
OF BOK KÖY

KURD HIKMET'S HAREM

The general tenor of my tales about the prowesses of the men of Bok Köy, a village situated on the marches of Eastern Anatolia, may well lead you to believe that all the young men of this remarkable community leave home at an early age to seek their fortunes in the great cities where they can find idle and wanton women. Yet many a dutiful son remains in Bok Köy to till the fields of a widowed and disabled mother, or for some other such worthy reason. Besides, it also comes to pass, every once in a while, that a boy grows up in Bok Köy who happens to be endowed, for mysterious reasons known only to Allah, with such great gifts that it is soon obvious that no merely human partner can ever be found to appreciate them. And who would ever set forth from home to become the mate of a monster?

In my own youth, before I left my native village to sing the praises, throughout the world, of the other men of Bok Köy, such a boy lived among us, a certain Hikmet, the son of a saddlemaker known to us as Ali the Kurd. Not that Ali was himself a Kurd, nor that he looked at all like a Kurd; but he had to be distinguished somehow from the fifteen other men named Ali in our village, and he thus became known as Ali the Kurd because he happened to beat his wives as systematically and regularly as Kurdish tribesmen are supposed to do. Nor did he lack good reasons for beating them. Ali was so remarkably built that his four legitimate hags were always malingering, claiming to be ill or pregnant, in order to evade their conjugal duties. Discouraged by such a constant sit-down strike in his own home, Ali soon developed a habit of disappearing from the village, every once in a while, in order to spend a few days on mysterious errands of his own in the mountains. Always, he returned from these errands quite obviously refreshed, and the whole village of Bok Köy began to suspect him of consorting there with a witch in a cave, until one day a calf was born, to one of the cows of the village *agha*, or headman, whose cattle generally spent the summer running wild in the pastures of the highlands. This particular calf, as it grew, developed an unusual gait, like that of a drunken wife-beater, so much like Ali's gait, on those nights when he had been drinking raki before returning home to beat his four wives, that the whole village was soon agog with new interpretations of Ali's mysterious summer absences on the mountainside.

Be that all as it may, Ali the Kurd's son Hikmet grew up to be even more powerfully built than his father, and it was soon known throughout the village that the boy, who had no particular reasons to stay at home, should be discouraged from going abroad in the world. We feared indeed that he might be caught there by slave traders, to be sold to Infidels who would probably exhibit him naked in a cage in a circus where idle and wanton unveiled women would pay a fee to gape at his monstrous gifts. Proud as we may be, in Bok Köy, of the gifts of our men, we are reluctant to see any of our boys shamelessly exhibited anywhere as freaks. So Hikmet was advised to stay at home, where the whole village would try to help him solve his problems.

A lonely and dissatisfied bachelor is always dangerous, especially in a small village. So Hikmet's friends and neighbors soon

50

began to seek, throughout the neighborhood, a suitable wife who might keep him out of trouble. His own mother and his father's other wives protested that no such woman could be found, but beggars cannot be choosers and we happened to have, in Bok Köy, an idiot deaf-and-dumb girl who was also an orphan, and she soon became Hikmet's bride without even realizing what all the fuss and ceremony might mean. The next morning, the whole village was curious to discover how the bride had settled down to married life. She emerged late in the morning from Hikmet's hovel, swearing like a drunken Janissary, in such obscene terms that all our women clapped their hands modestly to their ears and fled screaming. Hikmet's wife had obviously recovered, during her bridal night, her faculties of hearing and of speaking. Where she had learned her vocabulary of abuse remains, however, a mystery, for we villagers of Bok Köy are generally modest in our speech, so that the miracle of her sudden eloquence must be attributed to heredity rather than to environment. All that day she wandered round the village cursing quite shamelessly at all and sundry and announcing that if what she had experienced the previous night were indeed marriage, she certainly preferred to move forthwith to a great city and set up shop there as a career woman, in the oldest and only profession accessible to her sex. Late in the afternoon, she stole a donkey from a neighbor and set forth. Never was she seen again in Bok Köy, and Hikmet, on his return that evening from some errand in a neighboring village, discovered his misfortune, repaid the owner of the donkey, and settled down again to a sad life of celibacy.

A couple of years later, a cousin of the *agha* died, leaving a widow who was notoriously wanton and now threatened, in the eyes of other village wives, to disturb the matrimonial peace of Bok Köy. She was therefore married willy-nilly to Hikmet as soon as decency permitted such a ceremony after a period of summary mourning. She too, the day after her marriage, disappeared from Bok Köy for all time, but after declaring all day her intention of settling among the Armenians in the mountains and becoming a nun in one of their Infidel religious establishments.

Hikmet's third marriage proved to be an even greater source of problems and scandal. This time, a wandering Bedouin had chanced to drift into our village, half starved, with a starving child-wife and a brood of starving children. Few of us could understand much of his Arab jargon, and none of us knew, when he died two days later, whence he had come. What were we to do with his wife and his orphans? Hikmet suggested marrying her and adopting the children; the whole village approved his pious and charitable proposal. A few days later the ceremony took place. In the middle of the ensuing night, the village was awakened by a hubbub like that of an Armenian massacre: Hikmet's Bedouin wife had fled screaming, stark naked, out of his house and into the village street, where she fell on her knees at the feet of the first man of Bok Köy who emerged from his house to see what was up. Slim as all young Bedouin women are, she was a touching sight indeed, groveling there in the mud, naked as the day she was born, begging for mercy. What man could resist such charms? The fortunate man at whose feet she had chanced to fall picked her up, carried her into his house, and enrolled her forthwith in his harem as an apprentice concubine. The next morning, Hikmet felt obliged to defend his honor and was restrained only with great difficulty from murdering his rival. Deeply humiliated, he then left Bok Köy, abandoning the orphans whom he had just adopted, and it soon became known that he was roaming the mountains as a bandit.

But Hikmet was not made of the stuff of bandits and was in any case of a despondent nature. His banditry was moreover of a peculiarly unprofitable kind and seemed to consist mainly in the stealing of female asses. The number of she-asses that disappeared into the mountains increased steadily, and a herdsman once returned to Bok Köy with a strange tale: he had seen Hikmet in the distance, in the mountains, seated on a rock and playing love songs on a flute to a herd of fifteen she-asses that frolicked around him like Persian harem-ladies in the garden of an Isfahan poet-husband.

52

All went well as long as Hikmet's depredations were limited to the stealing of she-asses that belonged to friends, relatives, and neighbors. Unfortunately, he stopped one day, on the highway, a wealthy merchant from distant Marash, who was riding a milk-white she-ass and leading a whole caravan of loaded male asses. The merchant nearly died of fright, believing that he was about to be robbed of his whole load of rare Persian rugs, enamels, silverware, and contraband opium. Much to his surprise, he was deprived only of the milk-white she-ass that he happened to be riding. But this merchant was of a vindictive nature and immediately filed a complaint in the nearest city with the police, offering a reward for the capture of the bandit who had despoiled him.

What could the police do? They set forth and combed the mountainside until they found Hikmet, who offered no resistance, fearing that they might shoot at his beloved she-asses and harm them. He was arrested, ignominiously dragged to the city and thrown into prison. Our whole village took turns in visiting him there, bringing him decent food and seeing to it that he lacked nothing. When the matter came up in court before the Cadi, fifteen hundred inhabitants of Bok Köy were present to testify, one and all, that Hikmet was no highway robber and that the whole matter was a mere case of abduction. As the law states that true love is no crime and that Allah is always willing to intercede on behalf of true lovers, Hikmet was condemned to a minimal fine, after which he returned to Bok Köy and lived there happily for the rest of his days, a great poet and musician in our midst. We provided him, since such was his heart's desire, with a constantly renewed harem of she-asses, with which he also made an honest living as a transport contractor, carrying our produce from Bok Köy to Elazig, the nearest market town.

INTRODUCING ACHMET HODJA

Our village of Bok Köy seems to have always been destined to provide a setting for comedy, if not for farce, rather than for tragedy. We may well be, in that respect, a happy people, having never provided the world with such ghastly tales as those of Oedipus or of Hamlet. But even a happy people has, in spite of all that a French philosopher once said, some kind of history, and that is why our history has been mainly comic.

But comedy, though others may laugh at it, rarely seems funny to those who are immediately involved in it, and no cuckold, however ludicrous, has ever been known to laugh at his own predicament. The cuckolds of Bok Köy are in this respect no exceptions to the rule, as will be proven by the tale that I am now about to relate.

Not so many years ago, there lived in our midst a worthy merchant who, not being a native of Bok Köy, had not been endowed with the rare qualities that distinguish the male inhabitants of our village from those of all other villages in the world. On the contrary, this unfortunate man, a certain Abdi,

54

appeared to be a native of some village where Allah had been particularly niggardly in bestowing on the male population the kind of blessing that we men of Bok Köy enjoy. Be that all as it may, Abdi had foolishly settled in our midst, together with his four wives, as a result of the foreclosure of a mortgage on some property on which he had once loaned money to one of our native villagers. Unable to sell this property at a price that suited him, Abdi decided to occupy it himself, and thus lived in our midst, advancing us money on our crops, which he would then buy at absurdly low prices, and selling to us on credit, at absurdly high prices, the wares that he brought to Bok Köy from elsewhere. Soon, he thus became extremely rich, but a man cannot expect to be lucky both in business and in love. The richer Abdi became, the more notorious a cuckold he was too. For his four wives had not taken much time to discover the virtues of the men of Bok Köy and to make the most of their husband's frequent business trips, which allowed them to entertain in his home the *jeunesse dorée* of our village.

As these enterprising ladies became better acquainted with the male population of Bok Köy, they of course began to develop certain preferences. In this respect, they were particularly fortunate in finding that their immediate neighbor, Achmet Hodja, had every quality that they most enjoyed. Though scarcely gifted with appealing looks, he was a man of great vigor, endurance, and discretion, and it was much more decent to allow him into the house under cover of night, when he would be able to satisfy all four ladies in turn until dawn, than to give large and ostentatious parties for four or more men, as do the immodest wives of Americans, so I am told, in distant New York.

All this occurred many years ago, long before Achmet Hodja's unexpected Civil Service appointment as Hereditary Chief Eunuch of the Bath Towel in the Imperial Harem of the Sultan, an event which is related in detail in another chapter of the present *Chronicles of Bok Köy*. At the time when the incidents of the present tale occurred, Achmet still blossomed in relative ob-

55

scurity in our midst, like a rare flower on its native dung heap, though his virtues were already well known to all the gossiping shrews of Bok Köy. His relations with the four wives of his neighbor Abdi thus continued to be both enjoyable and peaceful for some time, attracting no more attention than his comings and goings with other hags and shrews of our village. With time, each one of these four wives indeed provided Abdi with enough offspring to prove that Allah wished him well, though Abdi's sons, thanks to the mysterious effects of environment rather than of heredity, were all endowed with the same physical gifts as all other native sons of Bok Köy instead of being as parsimoniously provided in this respect as poor Abdi.

Between his business trips to Elazig and to other neighboring towns and villages where he often had important deals to conclude, Abdi moreover enjoyed the friendship of his neighbor Achmet Hodja, with whom he played frequent games of chess in the only coffeehouse of Bok Köy, always winning each game and, though unwilling ever to lose, always teasing Achmet Hodja about his lack of skill or luck as a chess player and lavishing upon him the fruits of his own experience and skill. And so the years went by, quite peacefully, with the greatest cuckold of Bok Köy appearing to be the closest friend of the man to whose prowess he owed the misfortunes of which he seemed to be so utterly unaware.

Now there happened to be, among Abdi's numerous children, a daughter who was quite obviously no child of Achmet Hodja, being increasingly beautiful as she progressed from childhood to girlhood. Not that Achmet Hodja was at all aware of being afflicted with so infelicitous an appearance, the wanton and idle women of our village having for many years lavished enough attention upon him to give him good reason to believe that he was a veritable Adonis. He was indeed, by now, so deeply convinced of his own superiority as a male, even over all the other men of Bok Köy, that it never occurred to Achmet Hodja that a woman might ever consider him, in other respects, at all undesirable or repulsive. Be that all as it may, though discreetly paternal in his manner with all of Abdi's children, he yet began to treat this

56

girl, quite instinctively, somewhat differently; yet he would have been hard put to it for an answer, had anyone ever asked him why.

One day, when the girl was barely fourteen years old, Abdi returned suddenly from one of his business trips and, finding none of his wives in the house and all of his children at play in the village street, climbed up to the roof terrace to see if any of the women might be there, as women often are, either enjoying the cool of the evening air or busy hanging laundry up to dry. But the terrace was bare and, before going down again, Abdi chanced to look down into his neighbor's yard. There, to his utter horror, he saw Achmet Hodja busily instructing his lovely fourteen-year-old daughter in the facts of life while his own four wives enthusiastically watched the demonstration, lavishing their advice and encouragement on the somewhat puzzled child.

Furious, Abdi seized a bucket of cold water that happened to be close at hand on his roof terrace and emptied it upon the immodest couple and its audience in the yard below. A wild argument then ensued, which we must refrain from transcribing here in all its more lurid details of gesture and speech.

"After I've been kind enough to try to teach you how to play chess decently all these years, is this how you recompense me?" poor Abdi remonstrated. "Is that a way to treat a friend, to de-flower his daughter in the very presence of his four erring wives?"

"Sorry," Achmet Hodja replied laconically, "I thought they were all mine."

With that, the whole truth dawned on poor Abdi, who concluded that Bok Köy was no suitable home for an honest money-lender. Within a week, he had liquidated all his interests there and was gone, leaving us to provide for his abandoned wives and his numerous children, since they were all quite obviously ours rather than his own. But the men of Bok Köy are also endowed with great hearts, and none of Abdi's family ever had occasion, in our midst, to feel the pinch of want, though we were increasingly hard put to it to find, for his four aging wives, any truly useful or productive occupation.

HOW THE OFFICE OF EUNUCH
OF THE BATHROBE BECAME HEREDITARY

Need I begin my story by explaining to you who Achmet
Hodja was? His fame, whether as wise man or as simpleton, has
spread throughout the lands inhabited by the Faithful, all the
way from Bokhara to Fez, from Sarajevo to Timbuktu. Re-
cently, I have been told that some of the less ignorant among
the Infidels have already published learned dissertations, on his
divinely inspired blend of sense and folly, in the distant and be-
nighted universities of Upsala, Chicago, and Johannesburg. Let
it therefore suffice that I remind you that Allah, in His infinite
wisdom, had also seen fit to endow Achmet Hodja with physical
gifts of such magnificent proportions and remarkable endurance
as to be able to satisfy the lusts of the most wanton of women.
But these gifts, as if added as an afterthought to compensate
Achmet Hodja's many physical disabilities, were appended to a
person who, hunchbacked, crook-legged, prematurely bald,
hook-nosed, clubfooted, gat-toothed, and pock-marked, could
inspire, in every other respect, but repugnance and pity.

Be that all as it may, the rumor of this unfortunate monster's rare gifts began to spread as soon as he was old enough to become a subject of discussion, together with the other adult men of his native village of Bok Köy, meaning the Hamlet of Turds, among the nine hundred and ninety-nine mothers, sisters-in-law, mothers-in-law, wives, daughters, and sisters of this otherwise undistinguished community. Whenever these gossipy women gathered on the bank of the muddy stream to the foul-colored and sluggish waters of which the village owed its name, and began to launder there the cotton breeches of their menfolk, they would enliven their labors by discussing, as in all villages of the world, the stains found in their laundry, then also the qualities and faults of the men who remained, even absent, the main object of their concern. It thus came to pass, in time, that every one of these nine hundred and ninety-nine women of Bok Köy had been tempted in turn, out of wanton idleness, to taste in secret of the forbidden fruits with which Allah had seen fit to endow Achmet Hodja.

But not one of these nine hundred and ninety-nine wanton women of Bok Köy had ever fallen in love with Achmet Hodja, each one of them in turn using his services as if he were but a kind of public convenience placed discreetly at their disposal. Not even Achmet Hodja's own wife, a hag who in any other village of Turkey would have had to remain content with her broomstick, ever expressed any tenderness toward her mate. Instead, leather-skinned, hairy-armed, snub-nosed, flat-footed, foul-breathed, skinny-rumped and almost breastless as she was, she never missed an opportunity of reminding poor Achmet Hodja of his own unfortunate appearance.

Still, a boy had been born of this strange union, Allah-ud-din, a child that, remarkable as this may seem, grew daily in strength and beauty, the pride of the whole village of Bok Köy. In due time, it then became known on the riverbank that the growing boy had inherited his father's rare gifts, in spite of his not really needing such compensation for any lack of natural wit or beauty. But Achmet Hodja knew the nine hundred and ninety-nine shrews of his native village too well and was determined that his son deserved more worthy mates. He therefore devised, with his friend Murad Hakimoglou, a physician and the son of a physician in nearby Elazig, a strange plan to ensure Allah-un-din a great future in the Harem of the Palace of the Sultan in distant Stamboul.

Their plan was as follows. First, the physician would inflict on the boy's extraordinary gifts some quite harmless scars which might nevertheless give the impression that he had been made fit for a job as eunuch in a great harem. Then the physician would accompany him to Stamboul and, before presenting him to the Chief Eunuch for appointment in the Imperial harem, would also administer him a potion which would make him able to pass the strict Civil Service tests as if his scars, harmless as these were, had indeed made him a veritable eunuch.

The plan worked perfectly, as the conspirators had expected, and the boy was accepted in due course as an apprentice eunuch in the Sultan's harem. There, because of his rare beauty and charm, he was soon entrusted with the task of holding the towel or bathrobe when the Sultana in person took her daily bath.

In those days, the ladies of the Sultan's harem were particularly idle and restless. Many of them had been recruited from among the Infidels, so that their upbringing had neglected to prepare them for a life of dignified retirement. Affairs of state and other preoccupations moreover kept the Sultan from devoting to his nine hundred and ninety-nine wives and concubines the only kind of attention that might have justified, in their eyes, their rigorous seclusion from the world. Reduced to their own devices, the ladies thus played cards all day, consulted dubious fortunetellers, wrote poems, sometimes even studied theology. Several of them, especially the poetesses, had organized societies of mutual admiration where they discussed the uttter uselessness of men and had even discovered means of happily dispensing with the favors, rare as these were, of their Lord and Master. Others corresponded regularly with bishops and rabbis and other dignitaries of the communities of the Infidels and had already caused many of the Imperial harem's Moslem inmates to abandon the True Faith in favor of every kind of strange and foolish belief. The Sultana in Chief, a truly great lady, had developed a passion for contemporary French poetry. She wore at all times an emerald monocle, specially cut for her by a Frenchman who was then jeweler to the Imperial Muscovite Court, and she corresponded regularly with a chlorotic Parisian poetess who sent her autographed copies of privately printed limited editions of her works, together with autographed photographs which revealed "the Sappho of Argenteuil" wearing a cavalry officer's helmet, breastplate, breeches, and spurs, for all the world like one of the corseted military attachés of the Infidels attending in full dress one of the diplomatic receptions of the Sublime Porte.

One day, as this great but perverse Sultana was taking her bath, stripped of all her finery except her emerald monocle, she suddenly perceived, through this flawless green stone, an unusual stirring, like that of a captive bird, beneath the towel that her boy-eunuch was holding, spread out against his body and ready for the moment when she would rise from the perfumed waters and need to wrap the cloth round her exquisite and glistening form. A Circassian Princess, she was the daughter of a Mameluke from Egypt who had deemed her worthy of only the greatest of all living sovereigns, but this did not make her appear any less desirable to the common run of men. When she stepped out of her bath, the proud and beautiful Sultana simulated a moment of clumsiness in the course of which she was able to verify, with her erring and surprised hand, the exact shape, size, quality, and nature of the mysterious birdlike thing that she had seen fluttering or stirring behind the outspread towel. That evening, she summoned young Allah-un-din to her private apartment, ostensibly to fan her throughout the hot August night. True, no breeze reached the Imperial harem from the shores of the Bosphorus and even the fountains appeared to wilt from heat in the marble courtyards of the Palace. The Sultana and her boy-eunuch thus spent the whole night together in rare transports of love, after which she ceased to correspond

61

any longer with the Parisian poetess and even donated her autographed volumes of verse and photographs to the library of a nearby French convent for the education of the daughters of the wealthier Infidel merchants of Pera.

But the ladies of the great harem are not much different from the gossiping shrews of a village like Bok Köy, and it soon became known among them that the Chief Sultana had made the greatest discovery of her life, something indeed worthy of the attention of the nine hundred and ninety-eight other wives and concubines of the Sultan too. For a while, Allah-ud-din was kept very busy, but he was always able, thanks to the unusual powers of endurance with which Allah had endowed him, to give satisfaction to all and sundry. The Sultan began to receive reports, from the unsuspecting Chief Eunuch, of a most satisfactory lull in the harem's intrigues and of an unusual improvement in the morale of the strictly secluded ladies. They no longer accused each other of cheating in their card games, nor did they listlessly consult so many dubious but expensive fortunetellers. In their poetic societies of mutual admiration, organized on the same principles as the Courts of Love of the Troubadours who had once accompanied the Crusader armies of the Infidel in their assaults on our lands, the Imperial ladies no longer interrupted their debates to fight and tear each other's hair or scratch each other's faces, nor did any of them correspond any longer, on theological matters, with the sly and intriguing great doctors of the Infidels.

But this lull in the usual goings-on of a great harem could scarcely, in view of the very nature of women, be expected to last long. In time, several ladies fell in love with Allah-ud-din, each one of them wanting him as her own exclusive property. The Imperial harem then became, in short shrift, such an Inferno that the Chief Eunuch was prompted to conduct an inquiry into the cause of so much turmoil, after which he submitted a shocked but tactful report on his weird findings to the Sultan in person. He did this orally and in secret conclave with the Ruler of All the Faithful, lest the nature of the scandal he had discovered reach the ears of any court official of doubtful discretion who might report it all, for a consideration, to the special Constantinople correspondents of *La Vie Parisienne, The Sporting Times,* and the *Wiener Journal.* Among other findings, the Chief Eunuch's report included alarming statistics on the number of heirs whom the Sultan, who had not visited his harem once in five full years, had good reason to expect within the next few months.

But the Sultan was a sovereign of rare wisdom, busy with important affairs of state and too devoted to the privacy of his rare leisures, when he pursued other delights, to want his neglected harem to remain, at all times, a seething source of worry and vulgar scandal. He was grateful to the young eunuch for having solved, at least in the early stages of his career in the Imperial harem and within the limitations imposed on him by the lack of discretion of the ladies concerned rather than by any failings of his own remarkable potency, at least some of the problems of this vast and unruly hen roost. The Sultan therefore sent for Allah-un-din. Charmed by the boy's appearance and rare modesty, instead of ordering that he be impaled forthwith, the Sultan asked him to explain how and why he had thus been appointed under apparently false pretences to his job in the Imperial Household.

Allah-ud-din, like most country boys from the distant villages of Anatolia, was courageous, truthful, and respectful, and remained so in the presence of his Sovereign. Though dazzled by the magnificence of the Imperial divan, he did not hesitate to tell the great Sultan, in a clear voice and in modest terms, of his own father's misfortunes and of how Achmet Hodja had decided that his more fortunate son deserved a better fate. The Sultan was delighted with the boy's truthfulness and dignity and moved by the account of Achmet Hodja's fate. He therefore appointed Allah-ud-din, on the spot, Captain of the Palace Guards and then added: "Boy, send immediately for your father. I have important affairs of state to discuss with this Achmet Hodja. Why have I been deprived, all these years, of the services of so wise and resourceful a man from among my countless loyal subjects? Why do I always seem to be surrounded only by ambitious fools?"

Several days later, Achmet Hodja arrived at the Imperial Palace in Stamboul, weary and dirty after his hurried trip from the distant village of Bok Köy. As soon as he was announced, he was admitted into the august presence of the Ruler of All the Faithful, who gave orders that they be left alone in the Baghdad Kiosk, from the windows of which the view over the Bosphorus is truly like a glimpse of Paradise. In this exquisite privacy, the Sultan first assured himself that this monstrous old man, in his torn and filthy garb of a poor Anatolian villager, had been truly endowed by Allah with such rare concealed gifts of the body as well as of the mind. The Sultan then appointed Achmet Hodja Hereditary Eunuch of the Bathrobe, in Allah-un-din's stead, in the Imperial Harem, and then added, with a delighted chuckle: "Achmet Hodja, have you still a father as fortunately deformed as yourself, to inherit in the third generation this great honor, should your aptitudes ever fail to the point of suggesting that you may have reached the age of retirement?"

From that day on, there was no more theological strife, no more discord in the poetic societies of mutual admiration, no more argument about cheating at cards, no more trouble of any sort in the Imperial harem. The Sultan's nine hundred and ninety-nine wives and concubines took it in turns to be the joy of Achmet Hodja's days and nights, but not one of them ever fell in love with him. While strife of every kind now flared up suddenly, as if an evil spell had been cast upon the whole village, in distant Bok Köy, the Sultan's nine hundred and ninety-nine wives and concubines began to bear him peacefully a great number of beautiful and wise Princes and Princesses, all remarkably alike in their physical and intellectual gifts. True, one foolish Grand Vizir, a former Armenian slave who had reached high office through his gift for intrigue and gossip, was impaled one day for remarking to a Russian diplomat, in the presence of a loyal eavesdropper, that all these Princes and Princesses

64

looked suspiciously like the Captain of the Palace Guards. As for Captain Allah-ud-din, he soon became the Sultan's confidant, rapidly learning to unburden his Lord and Master of many wearisome affairs of state. He always slept, they say, fully armed on a Bokhara rug spread out at the foot of the Sultan's bed, the constant companion of the days and nights of the Ruler of All the Faithful.

WHY NAPOLEON ERECTED THE OBELISK
IN THE CENTER OF HIS CAPITAL

A potter who is a true artist in his work will never create two jars that are exactly alike. According to his materials or his mood, he must always vary the shape, the color, the texture, or the glaze. Allah, in his infinite artistry, can likewise never create two things that are exactly alike, and you will thus find that even the villages of distant Anatolia, however monotonously similar their immediate appearance, are all different in some way, if you only take the trouble to study them carefully. The village of Bok Köy, for instance, is named "Village of Turds" like many other such settlements built on the banks of a sluggish, malodorous, and evil-colored stream such as the Arabs always call Wadi-al-Hara, the River of Turds. But the village of which I am now thinking is on the right bank of the upper Turkish reaches of a Wadi-al-Hara that flows later through Arab lands into the Euphrates; and our particular Bok Köy distinguishes itself from all other Turkish villages of the same name in that its male inhabitants are endowed with quite remarkable physical gifts.

Many young men from our village of Bok Köy have thus wandered far from home and amassed great wealth in distant cities where the women are rich and wanton. One of them, for instance, went as far as Hindustan, where he lived happily and in great luxury, for many years, as the Prince Consort of a Sacred Cow, a curiously neurotic beast that, in a regressive mood, had developed a taste for the human partners to which it had been accustomed in a previous incarnation as a Roman Empress, a certain Messalina. But in ceasing to be human and in becoming a cow, the unfortunate Empress had also changed her whole proportions, so that only a young man from Bok Köy could now satisfy her nostalgic passion for human partners.

Be that all as it may, this tale of a young man from Bok Köy who became Prince Consort to a Sacred Cow may well be a legend, whereas the tale that I am about to relate is founded on historical fact and attested by a monument as well as by reliable chronicles and the letters and diaries of contemporary witnesses. It concerns, moreover, a young man from Bok Köy who, in relatively recent times, wandered from his native village in Eastern Anatolia as far as Al-Kahira, the capital of Egypt, before anything truly remarkable happened to him. He arrived in Al-Kahira, however, shortly before the occupation of the city by the French troops of the Emperor Napoleon, who had gone forth to conquer the lands inhabited by the Faithful and even proposed to set a live pig on a throne, as his Viceroy, in the sacred city of Mecca, should he ever occupy it too. Fortunately, mad as the ages in which we are destined to live may be, Napoleon never achieved his sacrilegious ambition. But, before being defeated in Egypt, he added to his personal staff, in menial offices, a certain number of the Faithful, among them our young man from Bok Köy, Muzaffer Özaltin, born of a family known for its great loyalty and therefore named Özaltin, meaning Pure Gold.

Menial as his tasks were, Muzaffer, who had to shine daily the Emperor's riding boots, soon attracted his master's attention by his modest demeanor and his loyalty. It thus came to pass that the Emperor, when he was forced to return to France, took the boy with him to Paris, to be a kind of decorative blackamoor at his court. In Paris, the boy soon became aware of the corruption of the Emperor's entourage. As the proverb goes, when the cat's away, the mice will play, and Napoleon was a cat who was very often away on his campaigns to conquer the world.

Muzaffer was thus able to observe that his Lord and Master's wife, the Empress Josephine, was a mouse of a particularly playful nature, the moment Napoleon's back was turned. But Muzaffer felt that the male mice with which she chose to play, when the Emperor was away, were scarcely of a kind that might be considered worthy of the only wife of so great a Conqueror. Besides, Muzaffer knew, from his own experience as a frequent clandestine visitor to certain badly disciplined harems of the wanton city of Al-Kahira, that he could successfully compete, even at his tender age of fifteen summers, with any paramour, whatever the latter's race or religion; also, that no Egyptian wife whom he had secretly consoled in the absence of a debauched and wine-drinking husband had ever been led to regret her indiscretions by having to present to her Arab husband a child born with the suspiciously round head and blunt features of our Turkish race, lacking the elongated skull and the sharp features of the Arabs. So Muzaffer began to play with the idea of defending his French Lord and Master's honor by becoming, in the Emperor's many enforced absences, the discreet and harmless paramour of the wanton Empress. But the Empress, being idle and wanton, facilitated his proposal by her own initiative, long before Muzaffer had decided on any specific plan of action.

It all came to pass as follows. In those days, the officers of the armies of the Infidels wore uniforms of a particularly immodest design, with tight doeskin breeches that left nothing to the imagination of the unveiled ladies of the French court. Many of these young officers, not being endowed with the physical charms that might ensure them success with the wives of their superiors and consequent advancement in their careers, relied on their tailors to supply them with artificial padding cunningly inserted in the proper places. One such officer, in every other respect a real broth of a boy, had attracted the attention of the Empress, who then summoned him, without further ado, to while away an afternoon with her, in her apartments, as her partner in a game of dominoes. On such occasions, it was Muzaffer's duty, shocked as the boy might be by all that he witnessed, to stand by and bring refreshments, such as Turkish coffee, whenever these were required.

All went well that day between the Empress and the young Captain, who already dreamed of rapid promotion to the rank of general, until the Empress, always very bold with her hands, made a surprise attack on her partner's more intimate charms. To her horror, her experienced fingers encountered, however, a mass that she immediately recognized as horse-hair instead of flesh. Laughing uproariously, she summoned Muzaffer and, to put the young Captain to shame, exclaimed: "I bet this boy is a better man than you!" When she reached toward Muzaffer to put her wager to the test, the boy thought at first that he would die of shame on the spot. But male flesh is in some respects weak, and he soon responded to the immodest caresses of the Empress, who expressed her delighted surprise by dismissing the Captain without further comment and retiring to her bed-chamber with Muzaffer.

Too humiliated by his own discomfiture, the Captain kept all that he had witnessed to himself. The French court only noticed that the Empress had become overnight more reticent, dignified, and modest, while at the same time seeming less restless, more content with her fate as an abandoned wife. Actually, night after night, Muzaffer lay with her in her Imperial bed, offering her until dawn innumerable satisfactions.

One day, the Emperor returned from one of his many victorious campaigns, too weary even to greet the Empress as any husband of so beautiful a woman should do on his return from the wars. But he soon noticed, in the days that ensued, what was afoot: his wife had failed to greet him with her accustomed list

69

of proposed promotions in the Imperial armies and, instead, his young blackamoor Muzaffer, whose demeanor remained in every other respect as modest and respectful as before, was now her constant companion and the owner of innumerable fantastic costumes such as the Infidels fondly believe that we Moslems wear on our daily rounds.

Far from being at all jealous, the Emperor was charmed by so much discretion. The poor man had learned, in Egypt, to appreciate the folly of women and the wisdom of our customs. In our more progressive lands the wives of great and powerful lords are quite properly housed like rare birds in harems like golden cages, to protect them against the consequences of their own wanton idleness, while the wives of the less fortunate among the Faithful are kept healthily busy toiling in the fields or weaving carpets. Unfortunately, the etiquette of the French court prevented Napoleon from supplying the Empress with two or three other wives and a whole crowd of concubines to keep her mind at work with the usual intrigues of a great harem, all properly supervised by a corps of trusted and experienced eunuchs. Napoleon therefore greeted Muzaffer's fortunes as almost his own, since they were obviously a lesser evil. The Emperor said nothing and, having returned to Paris for only a brief visit between two victorious campaigns, decided to devote his nights to much-needed and health-restoring sleep.

But it happened that the Emperor, like all usurpers, had many enemies among those fanatical noblemen who were still devoted to the cause of the exiled heirs of the deposed and beheaded French monarchs who had preceded him on the throne. Among these conspiring noblemen there was a former page boy of the beheaded queen who knew his way around the Palace well enough to escape notice if he managed to obtain admission there. Secretly, disguised as a member of the Emperor's personal guard, this man set out, one night, to murder Napoleon. He entered the Imperial apartments and was about to steal past the sleeping quarters of the Empress in order to creep into Napoleon's own room, situated further down the passage, when he

70

heard sounds, emerging from the room where the Empress lay, which led him to believe that the Emperor was there, fulfilling his duties as a husband. The conspirator therefore penetrated, with catlike tread, into the bedchamber of the Empress, and was just able to discern, in the dark, a male figure embracing Her Imperial Highness. In a flash, he stabbed the man whom he believed to be the Emperor in the back, with a thrust that would have killed immediately any man less hardy than our own Turkish boys of Bok Köy.

Infuriated by this interruption in his dutiful pleasures as much as by the pain of his mortal wound, Muzaffer merely turned his head, snatched the dagger out of his own back, and exclaimed, in the immodest and somewhat rustic terms of his native Anatolian dialect such as only camel-drivers use: "You scion of a long line of prostituted hags and unknown pork-guzzling fathers interspersed with an occasional mangey donkey, can't you see what I'm doing? Since when is it permitted, in this land of Infidels whose begetters are mostly unknown and whose mothers wouldn't be fit to empty piss-pots in a respectable harem, to attack a man while he is performing this sacred task?"

Horrified by this torrent of incomprehensible and guttural abuse, the murderer fled screaming from the room, woke the negligent Palace Guards, and was promptly arrested and shot. As for Muzaffer, he calmly continued to give the Empress her customary eight satisfactions, then rose, streaming with blood and scarcely able to breathe, from the Imperial bed; he picked up the bloody dagger that lay beside it on the floor, staggered out of the room and down the passage, then entered the Emperor's room, stumbled over a chair, woke the Emperor from his sleep, cast himself at his feet, and died there on the spot, begging forgiveness.

The Emperor was so deeply moved by the boy's remarkable endurance and loyalty that he determined to commemorate the incident, which had also saved his life, by erecting, in his capital, a suitable monument. He remembered that an archaeologist had persuaded him to bring back from Egypt at great expense an enormous stone obelisk that had never proven to be of much use. He ordered, the very next day, that it be brought forth from the warehouse where it had been stored, and he arranged to have it erected in a great square in the center of the city, without any inscription that might bring to memory the more ribald circumstances of this tragic tale. Today, innumerable elderly American lady tourists squint through their lorgnettes at this beautiful monument, without ever being at all aware of the great physical prowess and the tragic loyalty that it commemorates.

THE TURD THAT WAS AS BIG AS A HOUSE

Mother Djevrieh was only a half-witch, as good as she could also be evil, though nobody in Bok Köy could tell whether she was good or evil from the waist up or from the waist down, or whether her left side or her right side was better or worse than the other, her front more good or more evil than her back. Most of the time, she was no better nor worse than any other villager in Bok Köy as she went about her daily chores, milking her old nanny goat, gathering firewood, laundering, carding wool, or what-have-you. If one of the village women happened to be laboring in childbirth, Mother Djevrieh even turned out to be a real blessing for Bok Köy. Whether her skill depended on her intimate relations with the *djnoun* or earth-spirits or not, nobody knew; but she was by far the best midwife in all of our province. Whenever the Governor's wife was pregnant, he would send police to Bok Köy to bring Mother Djevrieh to the provincial capital and escort her back loaded with gifts, after the baby's delivery.

Mother Djevrieh's evil nature became apparent only when she lost her temper. Like a cloven foot suddenly revealed, her ability

73

to curse then left the whole village in awe. She would begin by cursing her enemy of the moment like any other quick-tempered village hag. But her curses, like music, soon began to follow a crescendo. From the usual curses of a hag she would progress to those of a seasoned Janissary drill sergeant; from these, in turn, to the curses of a veritable Infidel who has no respect for anything sacred. From then on, nobody in Bok Köy could understand her mutterings. Whether she uttered them in the secret language of the *djnoun* or in a foreign dialect that we villagers are too ignorant to understand, nobody could tell; but the sound of her mutterings became increasingly terrifying until she finally reached a monosyllabic oath that seemed to explode like a long repressed fart, after which she fell silent and senseless to the ground, her whole body twitching and her mouth foaming.

Her curses were effective too, but she always repented later of her anger and, inventing new spells, she also had a magical gift for transforming the disasters that she had caused into blessings. On one occasion, Mother Djevrieh had thus lost her temper, nobody could remember why, with Slim Ali's young wife, who was pregnant at the time. A few months later, the poor girl gave birth to a two-headed boy, which lived only to be six months old. You can well imagine how the young mother nearly lost her wits when she first saw her monstrous child, and how our whole village commiserated with Slim Ali and his family. But news of this monstrous birth spread far and wide. People came from all over the country to watch her baby sucking at both her breasts at the same time. The less credulous sometimes insisted that she strip it of its swaddling clothes to prove that its two heads, instead of being those of twins, were attached to only one body. For a while, the changeling seemed indeed to thrive. But it fell ill when its two heads could no longer agree to sleep at the same time, so that one of them was always awake and sooner or later woke the other with its cries. Never really sleeping, it gradually pined away.

Two days before the child's death, however, an envoy from the Sultan's Palace in Istanbul came to inspect the monster, offering its family a huge price for the privilege of bringing it up and educating it in the Palace to become a court jester, able to say "yes" and "no" at the same time and even to disagree with itself on fine points of philosophy. The parents accepted the money at once. When the child died two days later, the envoy had its corpse embalmed. You can still see it in the Palace in Istanbul, where it is kept in a big green bottle and causes the Infidel tourists to wonder whenever they see it rise or fall in the green fluid that preserves it, thus predicting tomorrow's weather for the daily press. In a way, this dead child has become Bok Köy's most famous citizen, in fact a world celebrity. To its parents, it brought a fortune. With the Sultan's money, they became our richest, most avaricious, and most oppressive landowners: may they now have a headless son, to waste their wealth and deliver us all from their clutches!

Mother Djevrieh's curses thus turned out, in most cases, to be blessings too, though mixed blessings since one man's meat will always be another man's poison and nothing in this world, except the Birth of our Prophet, can prove equally profitable to all men. Even the turd that was as big as a house, when Mother Djevrieh caused it to fall on our village, was at first a catastrophe to one family, then a blessing to all after being a mere nuisance to many. But as you all gape at my words as if I were inventing strange tales instead of relating what should be common knowledge, I must now tell you the whole story of the turd that was as big as a house, since I seem to be the only citizen of Bok Köy who is not afflicted with a memory like a sieve.

Mother Djevrieh lived in a hovel on the very edge of our village, as far as possible from the village pump where she daily had to draw water for her household needs. At her advanced age, this chore of fetching water from the pump had become the greatest exertion of her day. One day, as she tottered back to her hovel bearing a heavy bucket of water, some boys who were playing in the village street inadvertently kicked their ball so that it knocked the bucket out of her hand, just as she was about to reach home, and spilled all her water. Before returning to the pump to fill her bucket again, she stood there in the village street and began cursing the boy who had kicked the ball that had caused this annoyance. He happened to be the son of Durmush, our village miller. We knew at once that the village was destined to be afflicted with some new trouble, as if drought, bad crops, and rinderpest were not enough.

That night, as we all lay asleep in our hovels, we were suddenly awakened by a great rushing of wind that followed a crescendo, like Mother Djevrieh's curses, and ended as suddenly with a loud report like a thunderclap, followed by a curious squelching sound. Within the next few minutes, a terrible stench penetrated every nook and cranny of the village. To escape it, we all rose from our beds and ran out into the street, to discover that the stench came from there, in fact from an enormous turd that had fallen from the skies and smothered the hovel in which the offending boy's family lived, by the village windmill, which had been completely destroyed, as if by a witch's fart; and from beneath the ghastly mass of steaming excrement, we could hear the smothered cries of the miller's family as they pleaded for help.

All night long, every able-bodied man in Bok Köy worked hard with shovels and buckets to liberate the victims of this disaster and to remove to our furthest fields this stinking mass of manure. For days, our womenfolk then fought against a plague of flies as they swept and scrubbed everything within sight in order to rid us of the stench. A few months later, our fields began to yield year after year the crops for which our village has now become famous. As for the boy who had kicked the football which spilled Mother Djevrieh's bucket of water which roused her anger which brought upon us this mixed blessing, we all contributed to his studies out of the revenue of our increased crops. He was the first boy from Bok Köy to attend the school in the provincial capital. On a scholarship, he then studied in an American University, where he obtained his degree as an agricultural engineer. An expert in fertilizers, he is now our Minister of Agriculture, and will be here in Bok Köy next week, to make a speech when he unveils a bronze statue of Mother Djevrieh. Wait till you see it: like Lot's wife, she looks as if she's been frozen stiff, but into a pillar of shit!

76

III

ORIENT EXPRESS

MADEMOISELLE BLANCHE,
OR DIABETES CAN ALSO BE FUN

Mademoiselle Blanche Boissonaz was as unprepared for the adventures that destiny decided to inflict on her as a domestic cat for shipwreck in a maelstrom. All through her childhood and girlhood, she had lived in Villeneuve, a small town situated at the far end of the Lake of Geneva, where its waters are quietest and least stirred by the current of the Rhone River that flows through it and its air most rarely disturbed by the shrill protests of American secretaries from the World Health Organization when their bottoms are pinched, during their week-end leisure, by the cashiers of the Arab Bank. Near Villeneuve, the surface of the lake is almost stagnant, dappled here and there, beyond the reeds that grow closer to the shore, with huge clusters of waterlilies.

The youngest of the three daughters of a Swiss Calvinist clergyman, Mademoiselle Blanche knew only her home, a household which had become, in spite of her father's barely perceptible virility, a kind of parthenocracy. Her widowed paternal grandmother ruled the roost, scarcely less virginal in appearance and manner than the two unmarried sisters whom the unfortunate Pasteur Boissonaz also supported in his home; nor was his wife, in spite of her three children, any less virginal than her own unmarried sister, who had also sought refuge from an unfriendly world beneath their hospitable roof, soon after the death of Blanche's maternal grandmother.

Three unmarried older women and a widow who had experienced only four years of married life before her sickly husband died of diabetes thus imposed on the whole household the atmosphere of a kind of Calvinist nunnery. Inspired by its purity, the Pasteur and his wife brought up their daughters as if they might all three have been the miraculous fruit of virgin birth, produced without the rude intervention of a begetting father. Even their mother remained, after more than twenty years of married life, as "undeflowered" in many respects as her own unmarried sister and as her husband's unmarried sisters too.

Nor did this atmosphere seem in any way to frustrate the Pasteur, a meek and sickly man afflicted, since childhood, with the functional disorder which had caused his own father's early death. In theological matters, he was considered, by the Calvinist clergy of the canton, somewhat rigorous and even eccentric. It was whispered in synods that his womenfolk always wore veils over their hats, whenever they went on their household errands or otherwise appeared in public, because the Pasteur Boissonaz pushed Calvinist Augustinism to extremes of Africanist Puritanism and had thus imposed, even on his wife and his mother, the principles expounded by Tertullian, a Carthaginian Patristic divine, in his treatise *De virginibus velandis,* which insists that virgins should all be veiled.

But this expression of male authoritarianism seemed scarcely probable as the Pasteur's manner was anything but forceful. If the ladies of his household went abroad always veiled, it was surely of their own free will, an expression of their natural but almost otherworldly modesty. Seeing his own weak frame, his almost bloodless complexion, his mild manner and feminine gestures, one began to wonder how it happened that he himself refrained from veiling his features in public. Like a sickly child who had been raised with infinite care by an adoring mother, he had grown to be, as a man, more ladylike than truly effeminate. It was indeed a miracle that he had been able to summon up enough virility to marry and beget three children. Prematurely bald, afflicted with an extremely weak eyesight which made it necessary for him to wear thick lenses ever since childhood, permanently undernourished as a consequence of his strict diabetic diet, he survived thanks to the constant care lavished on him by the many women of his household. When the tiny spark of life kept smoldering in him all these years finally flickered out one summer night in his forty-fifth year, his presence was missed, by his eight surviving female relatives, like that of a harmless familiar spirit that had haunted their lives and kept them busy rather than that of a flesh-and-blood human being. At first, they missed him mainly because they no longer had to worry about his diet, though they still continued, for a while, to weigh slices of bread out of sheer habit and to keep a strictly calculated account of their own consumption of starches and sugar.

But they soon felt the pinch of his loss in other respects. Because the new incumbent of the deceased's ecclesiastical functions also had to occupy the house which had long been their home, they were forced to move to a tiny chalet on the outskirts of Villeneuve, where their restricted living space gave them the impression of being all too numerous as well as afflicted with too great a wealth of household goods. Gone were the days when each one of them had been free to enjoy the luxurious solitude of a room of her own. However much they tried to sort out their belongings and to avoid conflicts, they soon became as quarrelsome and intolerant of each other's peculiarities as if they were living out of their suitcases in an overcrowded railway carriage. Besides, the pension left to the widow of the deceased was considerably less than his appointments, slight as these had been, as minister of the Calvinist Church. It soon became clear to the eight ladies that they would never be able to live decently and

81

harmoniously in their new home on this pension and the tiny incomes that one or the other of the older women still drew from other sources. The three daughters would have to earn a living, if not in the somewhat limited economy of their native Villeneuve, then elsewhere in the wide and apparently unfriendly world.

The oldest of Mademoiselle Blanche's two sisters was, however, soon fortunate enough to find a relatively appropriate occupation in Villeneuve. The local pharmacist, who had already supplied two generations of diabetic Boissonaz ministers with a constant flow of medication that varied as biological and pharmacological science progressed, happened to have a pretty daughter who, since leaving school, had helped her father in his shop, working there as salesgirl and cashier. Suddenly, she had become engaged to a visiting English theological student whose cycling trip from his native village near Cheltenham to Florence, which he had planned to visit as an ardent admirer of the poetry of Robert Browning, had been interrupted in Villeneuve by a long bout of influenza and pneumonia, followed by a period of convalescence. After meeting for the first time in the pharmacy, these young people had gone together on a few appropriately chaperoned cycling expeditions as soon as the young theological student's convalescence permitted such exertions. A few months after his return to his home, he then wrote to Villeneuve, asking the pharmacist's daughter, whose virtues as a ministering angel he had learned to appreciate, to join him in wedded bliss in an Anglican parsonage in the Cotswolds.

It took little effort to persuade the good pharmacist, deprived now of his daughter's help, to employ Blanche's older sister, the pallid Gertrude. This solved to some extent the financial problems of the Boissonaz ladies, but still left their chalet very overcrowded. During the next couple of years, they managed to sell some surplus furniture by publishing somewhat innocently worded advertisements in the local French press: "Maiden lady seeks to dispose of old-fashioned but well-upholstered sofa. Ready to lose something on it." But then it was the turn of

82

Blanche's other sister, Claire, to venture forth. Having been raised and educated only to be genteel, if one can describe as gentility the almost spectral lack of any liveliness that distinguished the ladies of the Boissonaz household, Claire felt that her only vocation must be to educate the daughters of less refined homes to be as quiet, unpretentious, and undemanding as herself. Through a Calvinist agency, she soon found a post as governess in the home of a prosperous shipowner in Rotterdam. From there, each month, she sent a small sum to her mother, to help cover the expenses of their home.

When, a few years later, it was Blanche's turn to be likewise cast upon the mercies of an unpredictable world, the same Calvinist agency was again approached. This time, a position as governess in Turkey was offered, in the home of a retired Ottoman diplomat. Somehow, the older women of the Boissonaz household trusted that Constantinople must be more or less like Rotterdam, since it was proposed by the same Calvinist agency, and Mademoiselle Blanche was soon sent there, at the expense of her employer, aboard the Simplon–Orient Express.

The trip alone proved to be sheer torture. First, the poor girl had to share her sleeping car compartment with a stout and garrulous Turkish lady who chattered, ate sweetmeats and belched intermittently, without any qualms of conscience, whenever she was not snoring tumultuously in her sleep. Dressed *alla franca* all the way from Lausanne to the frontier between Hungary and Serbia, Aliyeh Hanum accomplished there a quick-change act, drew the curtains of the compartment's windows firmly down for the rest of the trip, had all her meals served in her curtained retirement instead of going to the *wagon-restaurant,* and appeared in public, if at all, only in full Turkish costume, heavily veiled. Her comings and goings, from her compartment to the toilet, caused a sensation among all the Occidental travelers in the same railway carriage. In their eyes, she heralded what lay in store for them in the mysterious Orient.

As for Mademoiselle Blanche, she was utterly cowed by this alien presence in her compartment. After crossing the Swiss frontier into Italy, she was even too nervous or self-conscious ever to venture as far as the toilet, at the far end of the carriage, except at dead of night. To reach the toilet, she had to pass, during the daytime, the open doors of too many other compartments and run the guantlet of too many idly staring eyes. All day, she sat in her compartment with her voluble companion, forced to listen to this strange woman's uninhibited confessions about the incidence of birth, copulation, and death in her life, or about the intimate details of the ailments that had now prompted her to seek the advice of internationally famous Paris surgeons.

"My husband," the Turkish lady explained with a touching pride, *"est très bien fait de sa personne.* He adores me, and I suffer the consequences of his passion. Well, you know, we women are subject to certain ailments. I can say with pride that I've earned my hemorrhoids the hard way. . . ." The Orient Express had reached Vienna and Mademoiselle Blanche had been treated to this account four times before it dawned upon her that her Turkish companion was actually referring to her husband's sexual aberrations.

In the dining car, equally shocking experiences awaited her. With the tact that usually distinguished the personnel of the *Compagnie Internationale des Wagons-lits et des Grands Express Européens,* the two ladies had been placed at the same table as two gentlemen of distinction, a monocled Hungarian Count and a bibulous English "Milord" who spoke fluent French and, to put the ladies at their ease, immediately ordered champagne, at lunch, for the whole table. Mademoiselle Blanche had never tasted this infamous beverage and nearly choked at her first sip of it, after which she felt a flush suffuse her neck and face; a few minutes later, unable to bear her confusion any longer, she fled back to her compartment without having eaten more than half her portion of *omelette aux champignons.* For the rest of the trip, she subsisted on tea and toast served to her in her compartment.

Such a restricted diet and such a regime of delayed bowel movements had reduced her, by the time they reached Sofia, to a condition of near collapse. Her Turkish companion was disturbed about her condition, but made matters worse by producing, out of one of her suitcases, a clyster and kindly offering to administer an emollient camomile enema. Mademoiselle Blanche burst into tears, interpreting this kindness as a ghastly invasion of her privacy. She began to wish that, like the angels, she were not endowed with any bodily functions at all. The last part of the trip, from Adrianople to Constantinople, was spent in an awkwardly brooding silence. Aliyeh Hanum had given up all hope of ever being of assistance to her odd companion. Her only fear was that Mademoiselle Blanche might burst like an overblown balloon before the end of their trip. Every once in a while, she increased the poor girl's anguish by suggesting that she loosen her corset in order to relieve its pressure on her presumably flatulent digestive tract. "You needn't be bashful, my dear. I'm armed to the teeth." Laughingly, Aliyeh Hanum would then wave her powerfully perfumed handkerchief, as if she were about to perform a belly dance; or else, from one of her purses, she would produce some *papier d'Arménie,* ready to burn it and purify the air of the compartment should Mademoiselle Blanche forget herself. Meanwhile, Aliyeh Hanum consoled herself by devouring pounds of Turkish sweetmeats, purchased at the buffet of the station in Adrianople, then belching immoderately as she fluttered her fan in the sickly heat of their compartment.

The Orient Express rolled into Sirkedji station after circling round half of the remains of ancient Byzantium, along a track that cuts irreverently through the ruins of the Palace of the Emperor Justinian. But Mademoiselle Blanche was blind to the grandeurs and the glories that had been both Greece and Rome, to the exquisite views of the Sea of Marmara, of the Bosphorus, and of the entrance to the Golden Horn. As the train slowed down, her listless eyes revived, to try to distinguish, on the platform, the wife of the Swiss Consul, whom she had been instructed to meet there.

An unmistakably Calvinist lady was standing on the platform, holding conspicuously in one hand, like a saint in the carved

85

portal of a Catholic cathedral, a symbolic object, perhaps the instrument of her intellectual martyrdom: a copy of the *Gazette de Lausanne*. In other respects, she looked like a governess or, in Switzerland, which exports governesses but refrains from employing them at home, like the wife of a *pasteur*. There was nothing at all elegant or fussy about her expensive but austerely sensible dress, a garment that seemed to have been designed for travel or pilgrimages rather than for diplomatic representation abroad. In Mademoiselle Blanche's eyes, Madame Cujaz appeared like a miraculous mirage of distant Switzerland. But Madame Cujaz was slightly shocked when this strange girl embraced her passionately and burst into tears.

Mademoiselle Blanche spent the next few days as a guest in the home of the Swiss Consul. At first, she could scarcely eat or speak and spent her whole day in her room or in the toilet. On the fourth day, she appeared to have recovered from the hardships of her trip and was driven out that afternoon, in an open carriage, to the *yali,* a palatial villa on the shores of the Bosphorus, where she was destined to be employed.

She was quite embarrassed by the warmth of the reception given her there by the bored Turkish ladies of her employer's household. Everything she wore, said, or did seemed to delight them. The moment she took off her hat, it was whisked away and tried on, in front of mirrors, by fifteen or twenty hysterically shrieking women and girls in turn. In exchange, she was made to wear a veil and brocade pantaloons while all the ladies of the harem shrieked again in chorus at her comic appearance. Finally, she was shown to her room, which she was to share with the two youngest daughters of the family, a child of twelve and one of nine, both of whom spoke a few words of French. As soon as the door of the room was closed, the oldest girl undressed and proudly showed Mademoiselle Blanche that she already had pubic hair. "You should be ashamed of yourself," Mademoiselle Blanche screamed, then spanked the child vigorously. Ten minutes later, Mademoiselle Blanche found the child weeping in their dressing room as she carefully shaved her pubic hairs away, as if it were a sin to be afflicted with them rather than to reveal them. Mademoiselle Blanche somehow felt that this misunderstanding was already symbolical of her whole future relationship with this strange family.

Still, the next few weeks remained pleasantly uneventful. Mademoiselle Blanche began to feel almost at home in these luxurious apartments, with their view of the gardens and on the Bosphorus. The ladies of the house were always alone, except when other ladies from neighboring houses called on them. Omer Pashah, the master of the house, appeared but rarely and briefly, spending most of his days and nights in the city. Though there were several menservants in the *yali,* they never appeared in the apartments reserved for the ladies. One saw them only at a distance or when they served meals in the dining room or on the terrace. When the ladies went into the garden, they generally wore their veils, and even the gardeners would suddenly vanish respectfully. At first Mademoiselle Blanche found this all very much like home, though oddly different, sometimes like a nightmare version of familiar surroundings. But she soon began to discover that, unlike the women of her home, these Turkish ladies seemed to spend most of their time thinking of men and discussing them. It all dawned on Mademoiselle Blanche in the course of a single conversation with Aysheh Hanum, the mother of the two girls who were her special charges.

Aysheh Hanum was a lady of great dignity, more reserved than the other women of the household. It had taken her two weeks to get around to having, with Mademoiselle Blanche, the kind of "heart-to-heart" that a mother generally has with the governess of her daughters. When she finally plucked up her courage for it, Aysheh Hanum went straight to the point:

"What kind of a man was your husband, Mademoiselle Blanche?"

"But, Madame Aysheh, I'm not married. . . ."

"Tut-tut, girl, I'm a woman of the world and I'm not asking you to produce your marriage certificate. But you're not a widow, so there must be some other good reason for your leaving home and choosing to be a governess in a strange land. I'm only asking you because I thought it would be nicer for you to bring up your child here. In a big house like this, one more, one less, as long as everyone is happy. . . ."

Mademoiselle Blanche burst into tears, torn between shame for her suspected condition as an unmarried mother and embarrassment at such broad-minded human kindness. It took her a long while to explain to Aysheh Hanum, between her sobs, that she was still a virgin and why she had ventured so far from home. Aysheh Hanum could scarcely believe what she was told: "What a strange country Switzerland must be! Why didn't they just find you a husband? Do you want me to find you a nice Turkish husband, perhaps a widower?" Mademoiselle Blanche declined the offer and explained that she had no desire to marry at any cost. She was perfectly content, if Providence failed to arrange that a suitable Protestant *pasteur* turn up, to remain unmarried for the rest of her days. Aysheh Hanum refrained from expressing her belief that Mademoiselle Blanche didn't know what she was talking about. But she became more and more determined, as the days went by, to see to it that this poor deluded Swiss girl should not waste the best years of her life without having experienced the joys of womanhood.

At first she sometimes thought that she had assumed here an almost impossible task. For a traditional Moslem marriage in decent Turkish society, Mademoiselle Blanche lacked the self-assurance, the natural feminine *aplomb,* that might ensure her her husband's respect. She seemed indeed to be totally unaware of being at all physically desirable. In any harem, she would be kept busy by the other women, sewing buttons for them and mending their torn finery, in fact reduced to the drudgery of a Cinderella. If her lord and master then appeared among his wives, Blanche would certainly find some excuse to miss the roll call and thus avoid ever enjoying her turn in the master bedroom. Obviously, she was totally unfitted for the competitive life of a polygamous home. Among monogamous Christians and Jews, Aysheh Hanum had too few friends to be able to launch

Mademoiselle Blanche socially without having recourse to trusted intermediaries.

The most trusted of these was Avakum Effendi, an elderly Armenian Christian eunuch who had long administered the estates of her mother's family before retiring to live in considerable comfort on his own savings. He was known, besides, to have good connections with the families of wealthy Christian merchants, many of whom were somehow related to him. Shockingly obese and afflicted with all sorts of infirmities, Avakum Effendi still made regular rounds to a number of aristocratic harems to visit the married daughters of his former mistress, partly out of a feudal sense of duty, partly too because he still found it profitable to undertake errands in the city for these ladies. Whenever one of them wanted to have a jewel reset, for instance, or to invest some of her savings in property, Avakum Effendi undertook the necessary negotiations, thus avoiding for the lady the possible humiliations of public appearance and of haggling over money matters with strange Infidels. In other harems, the fading glories of the Ottoman Empire, already known as "the sick man of Europe," were sometimes imposing painful economies when provinces and great family estates were lost in disastrous Balkan or Caucasian wars. There Avakum Effendi proved to be profitably helpful by discreetly disposing of such heirlooms as jewelry and rare carpets among his merchant friends. Aysheh Hanum decided to consult him about finding a monogamous Christian husband for Mademoiselle Blanche. She therefore sent a messenger to summon him from the city to her *yali*.

When Mademoiselle Blanche was invited a few days later to join the other ladies of the harem for coffee and sweetmeats with Avakum Effendi, she expressed surprise that a man should thus be received as a guest in their apartments. All the other ladies laughed uproariously: "Well," Aysheh Hanum explained, "poor Avakum Effendi is scarcely a man. . . ."

But Mademoiselle Blanche seemed immediately to find him to her liking. In spite of his obesity, he was no more virile in his appearance and manner than her own wraithlike late father. His birdlike voice was sheer melody to her ears. His hairless smooth cheeks, fluttering hands, and ladylike *minauderies* were all that she had ever hoped to discover in a man. Avakum Effendi, before he had been deprived of his manhood in an Armenian massacre, had moreover been a brilliant student in the French Lycée of Galata Sérail and even spoke fluent and educated French, though with a slightly lisping Levantine accent. In her honor, he managed to remember a few quotations from Lamartine's *Le lac* and expressed regret that fate had never permitted him to see with his own eyes the shores of her beautiful native lake. When he casually mentioned that he suffered from diabetes and must refrain from eating any of the sweetmeats that his hostesses offered him, Mademoiselle Blanche was utterly conquered.

"Quel homme charmant, cet Avakum Effendi," she exclaimed to Aysheh Hanum a few minutes after the good retired eunuch had taken leave of them. A few days later, he returned to the *yali,* though he had not been summoned. To Aysheh Hanum, he announced, referring to Mademoiselle Blanche: "What a delightful girl! Allah has sent her to us to be the perfect companion for my old age!"

It took some months to arrange for the mother of Mademoiselle Blanche to come all the way from Lausanne to attend her daughter's strange wedding in the Anglican chapel of the British Embassy in Istanbul, where no other Protestant church was available. Madame Cujaz had moreover expressed, in letters to the future mother-in-law, some tactfully evasive doubts about the suitability of this odd choice of a husband. But Madame Boissonaz, as soon as she set eyes on her future son-in-law, seemed to recognize in him some weirdly obese reincarnation of her late husband. And thus it came to pass that Mademoiselle Blanche became the lawful wife of an elderly, wealthy, and monogamous Armenian eunuch, in whose spacious home her whole family of Swiss spinsters and widows was soon happily reunited, all of them kept busy weighing slices of bread and keeping strict account of starches and sugar, so that Avakum Effendi's home had all the outward appearances of a somewhat puritanical upper-class Turkish harem disguised as a Swiss convalescent home.

A PATRIOTIC GIRL

Many years ago, our glorious Ottoman Empire, may its power last forever, was ruled by a Sultan, Abdul Mejjid, who had once been a strong and handsome youth, tall and powerfully built, but an utter profligate, the slave of his many whims and caprices. His excesses of the table soon made him repulsively fat, and his haughty manner, that of a spoiled princeling, could estrange even those loyal subjects who were prepared to revere in him the Ruler of all the Faithful rather than the fortuitous incumbent of great political power. Demanding of his retainers and partners a passionate devotion that his manner and appearance could scarcely be said to warrant, Abdul Mejjid tired easily of men as well as of women, and his personal household and harem soon attained such proportions, as a kind of luxurious prison to which he retired those discarded favorites who were fortunate enough to have survived his displeasures, that it began to cost the tax-paying Infidels of his realm more than our whole Army and Navy put together.

But this household and harem, as the periods of the Sultan's debaucheries became more frequent and lasted longer, actually began to rule the whole Empire. Nor was such a government contrary to the interests of the people, for every class and nation of our Empire was well represented there, as in a kind of parliament. Great Armenian and Greek ladies, for instance, took care, from the harem, of the interests of their compatriots throughout our far-flung provinces, while Arab, Circassian, and Kurdish princesses also saw to it that the regions which had been their native home should not be unduly oppressed by the governors who ruled them. *Alla turca,* a surprising substitute for Western democracy had thus been achieved, with checks of influence and corruption to balance all the excesses of incompetent tyranny.

One community of our Empire, however, was not yet represented at all among these many discarded or retired royal favorites; the Karaitic Jews who have lived here from time immemorial, ever since the Greek Emperors ruled from Constantinople before Mehmet the Conqueror stormed our Eternal City which, like Rome and Athens, is also built on seven hills. In the days of Abdul Mejjid, these Karaitic Jews, who speak Greek, who are wise enough to marry several wives as we do too, and whose wives, as ours, never appear in public unveiled, were no longer very numerous but still inhabited, on the shores of the Golden Horn in the Old City, a few dingy streets, between the bridge of Galata and the Rustem Pasha Mosque, in a quarter that had been assigned to them by the first Byzantine Emperor who allowed them to settle here.

Though the streets and houses where they lived had never been rebuilt, except for chance repairs, in close on a thousand years, many of these Karaitic Jews were great merchants who traded with their brethren of Al-Kahira, of the Crimea, of the cities of the Caucasus, and even of distant Bokhara. But they were modest and retiring in their habits, if not actually secretive, and rarely offered any of their precious wares directly to the eunuchs who were the purchasing agents of the Sultan's Palace. It came to pass, however, that Abdul Mejjid, may his guilty soul rest in peace, heard one day, from some Infidel boon companion of his nights of drunken debauchery, that one of these Karaitic merchants of our capital, a certain Kalonymos ben Aziz-ullah, had imported, through the good offices of a brother who traded with Chinese caravans in Bokhara, a rare Far Eastern simple, the powdered root of a herb which rejuvenates even the most weary and debauched of men. The Sultan decided forthwith to visit this merchant in person, in his establishment near the shore of the Golden Horn.

When the Ruler of all the Faithful appeared there, the hubbub and excitement caused in the narrow streets by his great retinue were such that all the women of the Karaites rushed to their latticed windows to observe the finery of the courtiers and the Palace Guards. As the Sultan entered the merchant's house, he espied, however, peeping at him curiously from behind an embroidered Bokhara curtain that was hanging in a doorway, the unveiled face of a little girl of twelve who was staring at him with dazzled and dazzling eyes of such rare beauty that he fell in love with her, or at least thought he did, on the spot.

Returning to his Palace with the coveted simple, the Sultan was unable to sleep all that night, his senses revived by the drug and his memory haunted by his brief glimpse of the Karaitic maid. The next morning, he called the Chief Eunuch of his innumerable harem and ordered that the child be enlisted forthwith in his army of wives and concubines and instructed to appear that very night in his Imperial apartment.

The Chief Eunuch hastily summoned Kalonymos ben Aziz-ullah, who turned out to be the father of the coveted child. Brokenhearted, the good man sought, in his distress, the advice of the *Haham,* or Grand Rabbi, of the Karaites, an old man versed in all the wiles of politics as well as in the lore that defines what is clean or unclean. Rabbi Theophilos ben Avakum Talalai, for such was his name, then decided that there would be no harm in allowing his community to be at last represented in the Sultan's parliament of present or past favorites who actually ruled the Empire, even if the selected deputy, since one could scarcely claim that the child had been elected, were forced for one night to kiss the lips of a man who was universally suspected of being addicted to eating imported German sausages, probably stuffed with the flesh and the blood of swine. The child was therefore entrusted for an hour to the Rabbi, who instructed her in her duties and explained to her how great an honor was about to be bestowed upon her as the most devoted and patriotic of the women of the Karaites. At the same time, he told her how she should purify herself after her night of self-sacrifice.

That night, the child awaited her Sovereign, in his splendid apartment, in mortal terror. When at last Abdul Mejjid appeared, staggering in his drunkenness, he threw himself upon her like the wolf on the fold. Properly instructed on how to show respect for her Sovereign, however brutal or unattractive he might be, the child was hard put to it to avoid weeping or screaming in her humiliation and pain. Unable to contain herself any longer, the wily girl, who had been educated at home by an Armenian governess, a graduate of the French convent school of Notre Dame de Sion, at last found a way to give vent to her mixed feelings in an appropriate manner and suddenly let out a piercing cry: "*Vive le Sultan!* Long live the Sultan!" After that, she swooned.

When she recovered her senses, she had already been retired to the harem, where she soon found herself in a position to obtain certain tax exemptions for her otherwise underprivileged co-religionaries, thereby depriving our Imperial Treasury of one more of its last reliable sources of revenue. To the Grand Rabbi, however, she sent, with her compliments, a magnificent crystal-and-gold casket containing a gigantic German pork sausage which she had carefully purified according to his own instructions.

THE SULTAN'S LITTLE HARUM-SCARUM, OR AN APOCRYPHAL SEQUEL TO "THE LUSTFUL TURK"

For his Imperial harem, one of our Sultans once acquired a peculiarly unsuitable young Infidel wife who yet turned out to be—for such are the devious ways of Fate—a veritable Godsend, for a while, to our glorious Empire. She was an English girl, the orphaned daughter of a professor of biblical archaeology at Oxford University, who had once been a very controversial figure in Anglican Church circles, where the fruits of his historical research often supplied ammunition to those divines who were concerned with what, in those days, was still called "the Higher Criticism."

This unfortunate professor, a widower, foolishly allowed his golden-haired child, then barely twelve years old, to accompany him on an expedition to the upper reaches of the Euphrates, where he planned to conduct excavations in a very wild and lonely region which he believed to be the actual site of the legendary Garden of Eden, though it had now degenerated,

95

since times immemorial, into an arid and mountainous landscape where rocks and ravines might remind one more readily of an Earthly Hell than of an Earthly Paradise. There, from the rediscovered kitchen-middens of our common ancestors, the professor hoped to recover fossilized human turds. Properly analyzed in a geological laboratory, these would subsequently allow dieticians specialized in the palaeontology of the quaternary to identify the undigested but petrified remains of whatever grasses and roots or nuts and fruits had provided the staples of the diet of Adam and Eve until they had both eaten of the Forbidden Fruit, which, of course, they digested and excreted elsewhere, after their immediate expulsion from the Garden of Eden.

In the course of this expedition, however, the professor's party was attacked by Kurdish bandits who raped and slaughtered them all, with the single exception of the distinguished archaeologist's golden-haired daughter. A natural respect for her tender years and for her market value as an unsullied exotic virgin prevented her captors from allowing her to witness the orgy and massacre in the course of which the rest of the party perished. Only later was the child told, by a village gossip, how her bespectacled and white-haired father had been disguised as a bearded Bedouin beldam and forced to execute a belly-dance in order to rouse the baser instincts of the rabble at whose hands he was destined to perish after satisfying their ignoble desires. Though the child was spared no detail of this hideous account, she never believed a word of it.

For the next couple of years, this future inmate of the Imperial harem was indeed kept closely guarded in a Kurdish mountain village, where her very identity was concealed, for fear of reprisals. Then, one summer, a dread disease infected the Kurdish tribe's flocks. Deprived overnight of more than half of their only legitimate riches, the tribesmen, unable to subsist on occasional banditry in an area that all wise travelers had learned to circumvent, decided to sell for a stiff price their only negotiable asset, the golden-haired virgin who lived in their midst.

Her name had originally been Gladys Tibbs, something both

meaningless to Kurds and difficult to pronounce. Her captors therefore renamed her Aysheh bent Hakim, having ascertained that she was the daughter of a man of learning, and it was under this new name that Gladys was now offered, through a number of reliable and specialized intermediaries, as a Kurdish Princess who would be a suitably beautiful and high-born wife for the Imperial seraglio.

Aysheh, *née* Gladys Tibbs, immediately saw in this audacious plan a rare chance to escape from the dreary social and cultural life of a Kurdish mountain village where nobody was at all interested in identifying the site of the legendary Garden of Eden or, for that matter, in any other subject that might have been discussed, over tea and mustard-and-cress sandwiches, in a learned Oxford drawing room. She indeed turned out to be far more co-operative than her Kurdish captors expected. She explained to them, for instance, that a recent French invention now made it possible to produce at short notice reliably lifelike portraits which, though gray because the camera was still color-blind, could subsequently be colored by hand. Inquiry then revealed that the great Paris photographer Nadar already had qualified former pupils, the brothers Abdallah, in Constantinople and Cairo, where they had been appointed "photographers of His Imperial Highness the Sultan and of His Royal Highness the Khedive." Brought to Constantinople by the intermediaries to whose care she had been entrusted, Aysheh posed for a photograph in the Pera studio of Abdallah Frères, after which her portrait was exquisitely colored by a miniaturist who was a nun in the Convent of Notre Dame de Sion, where she conducted art classes for the daughters of wealthy Infidels who are not forbidden by their faith to reproduce the human figure.

Because the womenfolk of the Kurds and of the Berbers are known, however modest in other respects, to reveal their features more freely than their Turkish, Persian, or Arab sisters, it was not considered unduly daring to communicate to the Sultan this unveiled likeness of his proposed bride. Other circumstances conspired moreover to crown with success the plans of

97

the Kurdish bandits. The Sultan himself, an enlightened monarch who had visited England in his boyhood, was now seeking a solution to the Kurdish problem, which was a constant thorn in the side of the Sublime Porte. He had thus come to believe that the addition of a Kurdish Princess to his staff of official wives might well serve as a means of assuring himself greater loyalty among her turbulent compatriots in the distant mountains of Eastern Anatolia. It thus came to pass that Aysheh bent Hakim, *née* Gladys Tibbs, found herself confined, far sooner than she had expected, to the strict but luxurious seclusion of the Imperial seraglio.

She had originally planned, in her ignorance of our Moslem marriage rites and of Imperial etiquette, to reveal her identity to the unsuspecting Sultan during their courtship, perhaps on the occasion of their first moment of relative privacy. Her English upbringing and her subsequent experience of the somewhat rustic and relaxed customs of Kurdish village life prevented her from foreseeing that, no sooner said than done, she would be the lawful wife of the Sultan on their very first meeting, so that she was quite taken by surprise when she discovered that her first moment of privacy with her Lord and Master was granted to her only on the occasion of her official bridal night.

She was prepared for this solemn occasion by a whole staff of Palace eunuchs, some of them hairdressers, masseurs, cosmeticians or costumers, others instructors in deportment or etiquette. The latter rehearsed her mercilessly until she had mastered every modest gesture, every coy glance, every tender word, and every passionate sigh that should accompany her voyage from maidenhood to womanhood. Never before had she seen such a fuss made of any event in her young life. Actually, she rather enjoyed all this flimflamflummery. At last, carefully coached and adorned, she was led into the Sultan's private apartments. There, as soon as the door was closed by an armed eunuch who would stand outside all night in order to watch over the safety of the Caliph of All the Faithful, she fell prostrate at the latter's feet and exclaimed, in her perfect Oxford English: "Your Imperial

Majesty must be informed, before it is too late, that His most humble servant's real name is Gladys Tibbs. I'm the daughter of the late professor of biblical archaeology at Oxford University! He was killed by the Kurds, on an expedition to find fossilized turds. . . ."

She expected this announcement, which was alien to everything that the eunuchs had so carefully taught her, to have almost miraculous effects on the Sultan. As a matter of fact it did, though scarcely those that she hoped to witness. Instead of promptly raising his supplicant new bride from the carpet on which she groveled and then magnanimously liberating her from her marriage in order to entrust her to the care of the British Ambassador, who would send her back to her long-lost Oxford home or to the girl's school in Eastbourne where her education had been interrupted by her accompanying her late father on his infelicitous expedition, the astonished Sultan exclaimed, with a perfect Oxford drawl:

"Tibbs? Did you say Tibbs? Are you the daughter of that old fool who instructed me in English when he was in Constantinople some twenty years ago with the British Archaeological Mission? Do you really mean to say that he was actually able to seduce and marry a Kurdish Princess when he finally left us to go on the expedition from which he returned a few months later with the fossilized rudder of Noah's Ark? You little harum-scarum, you can't make me believe any such hocus-pocus. Old Tibbs may be a wizard at identifying fossils, but he would never have been capable of begetting a beautiful daughter like you. And since when do Kurdish Princesses enjoy the privilege of being brought up by English governesses in their wild mountain retreats? There's something fishy, I admit, in all this, but we'll get to the bottom of it in due time, Tibbs or fibs, Kurds or fossilized turds. . . ."

Argue as she might, poor Princess Aysheh, *née* Gladys Tibbs, failed that fateful night to convince the Sultan of her real identity. The more she appealed to his better self, the more she confused him with her unlikely tale of woe. She even roused his

99

passions, till he finally insisted on enjoying his conjugal rights then and there with so beautiful and fanciful an English-speaking Kurdish Princess. Finally, she was forced to yield to his advances and soon became his favorite wife, partly because she was the only one who had ever resisted his demands and forced him to woo her, partly because he could chatter with her in English about a great variety of subjects that transcended the intellectual level of his other wives and concubines.

After a while, however, she managed to convince him of her real identity. To avenge her father, the Sultan then sent a military expedition which successfully pacified the bandit-infested mountains of the upper reaches of the Euphrates Valley, even recovering from the robbers the late professor's collection of rare fossil turds, which you may now see displayed in a glass case in our National Archaeological Museum, though some of them have also been sent, as a memorial to the martyr's scholarship, to the Ashmolean Museum in Oxford. But the Sultan and his pseudonymously Kurdish wife had meanwhile fallen in love. Instead of returning to complete her education in an Eastbourne boarding school for the daughters of gentlemen, Princess Aysheh, *née* Gladys Tibbs, had decided to remain, for better or for worse, in the harem of her Imperial spouse.

Whenever she entered her Lord and Master's apartments for their nightly trysts, he would now greet her tenderly as his Little Harum-scarum, after which they would reminisce a while about happy days spent in distant England, where the Sultan had spent a few summers as a schoolboy, to perfect his English. While he then boasted of his batting scores in village cricket matches or of his prowess as a fast bowler, she would talk nostalgically of mustard-and-cress sandwiches and of lemon-cheese pies served at garden parties in the rural parsonages of Oxfordshire, after which they would settle down happily to the more serious business of the evening.

In due time, the Sultana Aysheh, *née* Gladys Tibbs, thus became the real power behind the Peacock Throne, especially when she became pregnant and gave birth to a young Prince, unlike the Sultan's other wives who had all borne him only daughters. By that time, the Sultan's Little Harum-scarum had also come to the conclusion that her fate, however much it might have raised storms of protest or released cascades of tearful pity among unmarried feminists in Cheltenham or Leamington Spa, was much more brilliant than it would have been had she married a monogamous young Oxford scholar, as she once might have expected, in fact some brilliant disciple of her late father, a young archaeologist specialized in identifying the historical sites of somewhat legendary events related in the Old Testament. She might thus have married, for instance, the world-famous discoverer of Jephthah's daughter, buried in an urn on the spot where her heartbroken father had kept his vow and sacrificed her as a burnt offering after his victory, or the equally famous discoverer of the diabolical mandrake root which grew in the ground where Onan once impiously spilled his seed.

Though a brilliant young archaeologist's wife may experience great intellectual satisfactions in her conjugal life, when she dazzles her learned guests to a scholarly collation with Chaldean recipes salvaged by her husband from cuneiform inscriptions that he has deciphered on previously illegible tablets, the intrigues of a great Imperial harem can offer more scope to the intelligence and initiative of a woman who knows how to utilize her talents and wield her power with real discretion. Since fate had seen fit to grant her such power, the Sultana Aysheh, *née* Gladys Tibbs, decided that she would be truly foolish to refrain from using it, not so much to her own advantage as to that of her sex and of mankind at large.

Her education, before her Kurdish adventures, had not been neglected. In addition to a good basic knowledge of English constitutional history as explained by Walter Bagehot, she was endowed with sound political notions of her own. On the whole, her ideas were moderately progressive. She had read most of the published novels of Charles Dickens and even *Adam Bede*. Seeking a historical example to inspire and guide her in her self-appointed mission, she was wise enough to understand the peculiarities of her own situation and, instead of setting out to imitate in her actions those of some feminist termagant, she preferred to choose as her model Prince Albert of Saxe-Coburg-Gotha who, as Prince Consort, so often inspired the wise decisions for which Queen Victoria was destined to be remembered by several generations of her nostalgic and grateful subjects.

More and more, the Sultana Aysheh, *née* Gladys Tibbs, now discussed politics with her Lord and Master. Sometimes, he would heave sighs of boredom as he listened to her; often, at first, he would interrupt her by playfully pinching her shapely bottom in order to recall her to her more pleasurable wifely duties. Still, she seemed to derive healthy satisfactions from these too. Little by little, the Sultan learned to appreciate her political acumen and began to come to her for advice in solving some of the problems of his far-flung Empire. Their Imperial evenings would then be spent discussing the latest editorial of the London *Times,* which speculated on how the Sublime Porte would respond to a recent diplomatic move of the Ballhausplatz, or on whether "the Sick Man of Europe" would be able to withstand some new military pressure of the Russian Steamroller in the Balkans or the Caucasus; after which, having solved at least in theory the problems of the day, the Sultan and his Little Harum-scarum would settle down to such lighter pastimes as an old-fashioned Cockney "slap and tickle" or, if they needed first to rouse their appetites, to a joint reading of *The Lustful Turk* or of an English translation of a French classic of its kind, *The Memoirs of a Masseuse.*

All too often, the Gallicisms of the latter, which had been hurriedly translated by a slovenly hack, perplexed them and led them astray, in the *selva oscura* of philological speculation. One night, they thus devoted several desultory hours to an *explication de texte,* trying to visualize what might well be meant by the following cryptic paragraph: "In the confusion that ensued, he gamahuched the Duchess behind a palm tree in the conservatory, then begged her to order her footmen to flog him for having failed to respect her. She complied with his wishes, but in-

102

sisted that he should also gamahuche Ann, her French maid, which he proceeded to do in the presence of the whole household while he was being roundly chastised for the liberties he was taking. Unperturbed, the Duchess watched us through her lorgnette. . . ."

Gamahuched? The Imperial lovers racked their memories of classical philology and of several contemporary foreign languages without being able to understand what might well be meant by this cryptic word, neither Latin nor Germanic and probably Celtic, in the *Memoirs of a Masseuse*. Then, a few days later, the Sultan's Little Harum-scarum coyly announced to her Lord and Master that she had solved the riddle. Among the other ladies of the Imperial seraglio, she had discovered a long-dead Sultan's former Armenian concubine, an elderly lady who, having previously been educated by the French nuns of Notre Dame de Sion, had developed a taste for advanced French poetry and thus chanced upon this curious word in a somewhat more explicit context, in fact in one of the poems of Paul Verlaine's *Hombres*. When the Sultana Aysheh, *née* Gladys Tibbs, now explained blushingly to the Sultan how he could gamahuche her like any English Duchess or French maid, his Imperial Highness was as surprised as Monsieur Jourdain discovering, in Molière's *Le Bourgeois Gentilhomme,* that what he had just been taught to call "prose" was exactly what he had always been speaking. But a rose, by a new name, can smell much sweeter; and the Imperial couple henceforth gamahuched all the more gleefully.

But this philological episode proved to be the source of sweeping reforms in the Imperial harem. It occurred to the Sultana Aysheh, *née* Gladys Tibbs, that its numerous ladies wasted all too much of their talents and time on idle occupations, endlessly filing their nails, plucking their eyebrows, playing patience, reading the future from tea leaves or mooning over French novels of dubious intellectual value. With the approval of her Imperial Lord and Master, the Sultana Aysheh now put them all to work reading the foreign press and drafting intelligence reports. From the nights that he now spent with his Little Harum-scarum, the Sultan returned increasingly refreshed in mind as well as in body. In the audiences that he gave on the morrow, whether to his own Viziers, to foreign diplomats, or to petitioners from every class among his subjects, the decisions that he took and the judgments that he pronounced soon began to earn him throughout the world the reputation of a modern Solomon. To the dismayed Russian Ambassador, he would quote, with a faint note of sarcasm, what the editorial of the London *Times* had recently suggested that a somewhat less debilitated "Sick Man of Europe" might still do to save from Tsarist colonialism some threatened Caucasian or Balkan province of our dwindling Empire. To the equally surprised English Ambassador, he would almost absentmindedly mention the latest London Stock Exchange quotations for Suez Canal shares, thus revealing that he too had been wisely nibbling at the hard-pressed Egyptian Khedive's fabulous holdings of this stock which Prime Minister Disraeli, through his Rothschild connections, was seeking to acquire *en bloc* and at a discount for the British Crown.

But the Imperial harem soon found itself understaffed as a camouflaged intelligence agency, and the Sultana Aysheh, *née* Gladys Tibbs, was forced to seek ways and means of recruiting new talent for its rapidly expanding activities. Increasingly staffed with bespectacled blue-stockings recruited from among the underemployed feminists of all Western nations, it was rapidly loosing much of its glamor as a legendary abode of odalisques and houris. In London, the Realist novelist George Gissing, seeking in the Main Reading Room of the British Museum the real-life material that he could use in *The New Grub Street,* began to observe that this great reservoir of exploited female intellectual talent was already haunted by far fewer "odd women" of the kind that generally eke out a meager subsistence there as "ghosts" for more eminent male scholars. On the other hand, the halls of such learned clubs as the Athenaeum were more and more deserted as their members, for lack of female help, were increasingly reduced to doing their own dreary spadework in the Main Reading Room of the British Museum. In Moscow and Saint Petersburg, the ranks of those feminist Nihilists whose activities the great novelist Joseph Conrad has so well described in *Under Western Eyes* were likewise thinning. Fewer of them could now be found to conceal time-bombs beneath their bustles and, in a flurry of hastily raised petticoats, to bowl them unerringly into the passing carriages of reactionary Ministers of Police. In the emergency, a new kind of miniaturized time-bomb had to be devised, small enough to be concealed in a man's bowler hat. In Vienna, the more intellectual Catholic orders were experiencing difficulty in recruiting novices for their convents among the convert daughters of titled Jewish bankers. In Paris, slim volumes of Symbolist poems published on green paper by Lesbian poetesses at their own expense became increasingly scarce. From all over Europe, a secret network of Turkish agents was indeed recruiting young women of education, intelligence, and talent for our Sultan's harem, where they were immediately put to work reading newspapers and more specialized periodicals or writing press reviews and intelligence reports, but in far greater comfort and luxury than they had previously known in the British Museum, in the Bibliothèque Nationale or elsewhere. As for our Sultan, the Ruler of All the Faithful, he was now the best-informed of all Caliphs since Haroun-al-Rashid, in fact the wisest of all living monarchs.

Almost overnight and by purely peaceful means, the "Sick Man of Europe" was becoming a great progressive power, feared and respected in Whitehall, by the Ballhausplatz, the Quai d'Orsay, the Wilhelmstrasse, and on the banks of the Neva. When a British engineer invented the submarine and failed to interest the First Lord of the Admiralty in its usefulness as a guarantee of world peace, the diligent bespectacled odalisques of our Imperial seraglio promptly brought the matter to the attention of our Sultan; and so it came to pass that the Imperial Turkish Navy was the first in the world to order and commission submarines. In France, our political propaganda brought about a literary revolution: working on our secret payroll, the popular novelist Pierre Loti deliberately gave his foolish readers the false impression that the ladies of our harems had nothing better to do than to entertain him secretly to coffee, idle talk, and *rahat loukoum*. For a while, the Quai d'Orsay thus continued to believe that it could successfully undermine our authority among the Christians of Syria and Lebanon.

But our moral rearmament as a great power was thwarted all too soon by the sinister intrigues of our imperialist enemies. Puzzled at first by a secret drain on England's female intelligence that was already threatening the future of the English novel and diverting younger bluestockings from the goose-quill pens which made George Eliot and Mrs. Gaskell world-famous, Scotland Yard began to watch more carefully the activities of our agents who were so busy recruiting talent for the Imperial harem. Oddly enough, these agents, unlike their fictional colleagues in that hoary classic of English erotic fantasy, *The Lustful Turk,* seemed to lay no store by good looks, nor indeed by unsullied virtue; indeed, the passport to employment, wherever these young women vanished, appeared to be intelligence and experience rather than innocence and beauty. Yet those who could be traced after their disappearance all wrote from the same Imperial palaces built on the shores of the Golden Horn or the Bosphorus, from Top Kapou, Dolmah Bahtche, Beylerbey, or Yildiz. Our Sultan thus began to be suspected of having very peculiar tastes and of being the only client of a white slave traffic of an entirely novel kind.

To uncover its methods and purposes, Scotland Yard soon found a suitable agent: Miss Gwendolen Trollope, an unemployed elderly lady archaeologist of formidable appearance who, for many years, had been reader and research assistant to the late Professor Tibbs and, since his mysterious disappearance, was living in penurious retirement in a boardinghouse in Bloomsbury. She was promptly put to work in the British Museum Reading Room where, to attract the attention of the mysterious recruiters, she was instructed to read assiduously the more learned publications of the Prussian Academy of Arts and Sciences. Within a week, Miss Gwendolen Trollope was approached by a mild-mannered Dissenting clergyman and vanished too.

In a recognition scene similar to that, in classical tragedy, where Orestes suddenly finds himself about to be sacrificed, in the temple of Tauris, by his own long-lost sister Iphigenia, the Sultana Aysheh, *née* Tibbs, found herself facing, a few weeks later, her own late father's former research assistant, when Miss Gwendolen Trollope turned up as a Trojan horse, in fact disguised as a new recruit for the Imperial harem's secret corps of information specialists. Little did the Sultana suspect, at the time, what troubles would soon be brewing, though she wisely refrained from revealing to Miss Trollope her real identity.

Prepared for the very worst and ready to sacrifice her all for the future of England, Miss Trollope was convinced that she was doomed, in spite of her age and her appearance, which had never been at all enticing, to meet at the hands of the Sultan the fate that, in the eyes of most English women, is worse than death, in fact the kind of delicious humiliation that is so well described again and again in the pages of *The Lustful Turk,* which she had managed to consult, in the Inferno of the British Museum Library, before setting forth on her perilous mission. As the weeks went by without her yet having had to submit to any humiliation of the kind that she both feared and ardently desired, she began to regret her Bloomsbury boardinghouse, the British Museum Main Reading Room, in fact her whole drab life of penurious retirement from which she had escaped to this veritable hive of intellectual activity. Politics had never interested her. Under the scholarly guidance of Professor Tibbs, she had exercised her intellect on problems of an entirely different nature. Originally an amateur collector of geological specimens culled during her girlhood holidays in Wales, in the Lake District, or the Trossachs, she had gradually become an expert in fossilized ferns, petrified woods, and other such prehistoric curiosities. Actually, she could pride herself on having been the one who had originally opened the eyes of Professor Tibbs to the inherent scientific possibilities of fossilized human turds or coproliths as clues to the diet of prehistoric man.

107

Reports on Austrian troop movements in Bosnia and Herze-
govina left her cold. Her idle emotions began to crystallize in
the most peculiarly violent resentments, which she even had the
courage to voice among her colleagues. Within a few months,
Miss Gwendolen Trollope thus became the leader of a move-
ment for feminine rights among the less satisfied bluestockings
of the Imperial harem who felt that the Sultan was neglecting
them as wives or concubines. After all, they had abandoned the
monogamous world of the West and adopted the Moslem way of
life, but without yet having enjoyed the more tangible advan-
tages of polygamy. Their murmurs were soon voiced as overt
complaints. With the eloquence of a dedicated suffragette leader,
Miss Gwendolen Trollope managed to rouse her followers to a
real frenzy. One day, when the Sultan was passing through the
main reading-room of his seraglio, accompanied by the Sultana
Aysheh, *née* Tibbs, a group of infuriated and bespectacled
lady scholars, led by Miss Gwendolen Trollope, suddenly rose
from their desks and rushed at him, like the Maenads attack-
ing Orpheus. In their desperate fight to be joined with him
in carnal union, they tore the unfortunate Ruler of All the
Faithful limb from limb, trampling to death his faithful Little
Harum-scarum, who sought in vain to protect the poor Turk
from this wild band of lustful Englishwomen.

Scotland Yard, the Foreign Office, and the Colonial Office
had thus won their battle to protect the land route to India
against any recovery of the "Sick Man of Europe" as a major
political power. In the Honors List that Prime Minister Disraeli
proposed to Queen Victoria that year on the occasion of Her
Majesty's Birthday, Miss Gwendolen Trollope was the first
woman to be awarded the title of Dame of the British Empire.

But Miss Gwendolen Trollope was no longer of this world to
enjoy such honors. The Palace Guards, alarmed by the turmoil,
had rushed into the harem, though too late to protect their Sov-
ereign. They had then arrested the ringleader of the revolt, to-
gether with her whole band of rebels. Summarily tried, they were
all condemned to be disposed of in a manner which, however
barbarous it may seem, has traditionally proven effective as a

means of silencing rebellious wives. Each one of them was placed in a stout barrel lined with iron spikes. Over one hundred of these barrels were then allowed to roll down the hills of Bebek into the Bosphorus.

From the heights where the Americans subsequently built Roberts College, the Captain of the Palace Guard was able to see that all the barrels sank into the waters, with one exception, which proved that its inmate was a witch. Floating into the Sea of Marmara and then through the Hellespont into the Aegean Sea, this barrel subsequently drifted all the way across the Mediterranean to Gibraltar, where it was salvaged as flotsam and jetsam, in fact as property of Her Majesty the Queen. When it was opened, it was found to contain the miraculously pickled and preserved remains of Gwendolen Trollope, a posthumous Dame of the British Empire. Two years after her disappearance, she was indeed identified by the fossilized human turd which, mounted in gold as a pendant, she still wore on a chain round her neck: a famous Bond Street jeweler was able to testify that it was the only bauble of its kind, having been specially made for her, with her initials inscribed in its gold setting, as a gift from the late Professor Tibbs, shortly before his mysterious disappearance. In addition, the lorgnette that was found intact in a rotting leather case in the same barrel proved to have been made for Miss Gwendolen Trollope by a reputable firm of Regent Street opticians, who testified that she was the only one, among their many clients, to have ever required this particular prescription. Like most witches, not only did she float on water instead of sinking like any honest woman, but she had also been for many years an optometrical freak, shortsighted in one eye and farsighted in the other, in fact swivel-eyed enough to have attracted the attention not only of Scotland Yard but of Satan himself.

Note: The authorship of The Lustful Turk, *ever since its first anonymous publication in London in 1818, has again and again inspired research and speculation among specialists of nineteenth-century English fiction. A felicitous recent discovery, in the somewhat chaotic archives of the Sub-*

lime Porte, now allows us to solve all the problems posed by the authorship of this remarkable novel. As everyone knows, the enemies of our Empire had agreed in 1817 to stamp out the activities of our galant privateers who, for centuries, had been zealously liberating unfortunate Christian women from the slavery to which they are generally condemned in their native lands. I need but refer the interested reader to such realist classics as John Cleland's Fanny Hill: The Memoirs of a Woman of Pleasure, George Moore's Esther Waters, and Stephen Crane's Maggy, or a Girl of the Streets; these books all prove that a woman's life, even in relatively modern times, has not always been a bed of roses among the Infidels.

Be that as it may, an English fleet commanded by Lord Exmouth bombarded Algiers in 1817 and forced its Dey, who was a vassal of our Sultan, to hand over some three thousand refugees, including several hundred foreign women who had found happiness in the Dey's harem. As is usual in such cases, many of these "liberated" foreigners were then prevailed upon to publish lurid accounts of their experiences in their Moslem "captivity." The more horrifying these pseudographical memoirs, the more widely they were read.

To put an end to so much malicious anti-Turkish propaganda, our Sultan instructed our Ambassador to the Court of Saint James to approach a talented English writer who might be prevailed upon to give a more truthful picture of the life of the privileged inmates of an aristocratic Moslem harem. The great novelist Jane Austen dickered with the idea, but subsequently refused the assignment, arguing that she had too little experience of these matters to be able to write about them convincingly. Sir Walter Scott was too busy, or else too chauvinistic. The Reverend Robert Maturin, the immortal author of Melmoth the Wanderer, accepted the task, but soon abandoned it under the pressure of ill-health, which led to his untimely death in 1824. His unfinished manuscript thus fell into the hands of S——— J———, Esq., who claimed, in the first edition of the book, to be of Magdalen College, Oxford.

In its present version, The Lustful Turk still includes a series of letters, from Pedro to Angelo and from Angelo to Pedro, which were obviously written by the Reverend Maturin who, here as well as in Melmoth the Wanderer, could not refrain from giving voice to his anti-Catholic prejudices, even if he had now been commissioned to defend the interests of Islam. But the rest of The Lustful Turk is entirely the work of this mysterious S——— J———, Esq.; one need but read his descriptions of love scenes to realize that he was a masochistic passive homosexual who allowed his own erotic fantasies to dictate to him a number of unrealistic episodes, though our Ambassador had originally given to the Reverend Maturin sufficiently detailed testimony, from inmates of our harems, to allow the author of the proposed work to present a more realistic picture of our customs.

When The Lustful Turk was finally published in its present form, its presumptuous author had the audacity to approach our Ambassador with a request for payment, claiming that he had completed the Reverend

Maturin's task but had not inherited from the latter, together with his unfinished manuscript, any of the sums advanced in order to encourage him to concentrate all his talents on this important and confidential work.

Our Ambassador read The Lustful Turk *and was sensible enough to perceive that the book, in its present form, could only do our cause more harm than good. He answered the author's letter with the wisdom of a veritable King Solomon: he suggested that he might consent to pay for part of the book, if the Pope could also be prevailed upon to pay for the writing of the letters exchanged between Angelo and Pedro. And there the matter seems to have rested.*

All this correspondence, between our Ambassador and the various above-mentioned English authors, including the mysterious S———— J————, Esq., who claimed to be of Magdalen College, Oxford, has now come to light in our Imperial Archives. S———— J———— proves to be a certain Silas Jenkins, a notorious London hack, perhaps even a superannuated male prostitute, whose only knowledge of life in an Oriental palace seems to have been gleaned from his early apprenticeship as an assistant to the Prince Regent's notoriously homosexual chief cook in the Brighton Pavilion! As for his connection with Magdalen College, it was tenuous: Silas Jenkins had married a former prostitute and now lived mainly, since his talents failed to feed him, on what she had saved, as a kind of new Mary Magdalene, from the immoral earnings of her ill-spent youth.

A MEEK WOLF AMONG SAVAGE LAMBS

In the early and happier years of the reign of our late Sultan Abdul Hamid, may his sick and troubled soul rest in peace, it suddenly became fashionable among the more idle and wealthy Infidels to visit our glorious capital. Overnight, great trains, real caravanserais on wheels with bedrooms, bathrooms, and restaurants installed in their carriages, began to unload almost daily, on the platforms of Sirkeji Station, the oddest crowds of monocled and side-whiskered gentlemen accompanied by their unveiled womenfolk, who wore dead birds on their heads and had the voices of petulant screech owls. All of them were intent, in a frenzy of indecent curiosity, on violating what they believed to be the lascivious mysteries of our enigmatic Orient.

News of this relatively peaceful invasion soon penetrated the harems of the more elegant *yalis,* or waterfront villas, inhabited, along the shores of the Bosphorus, by the great Ottoman families. In the absence of their husbands, most of whom now played poker all day in the lounges of the Pera Palace Hotel in the new Beyoglu quarter of Istanbul, some idle and frivolous Turk-

112

ish ladies began to organize tea parties, known in the French they had learned from the nuns of Notre Dame de Sion as *"le five o'clock,"* in the course of which they entertained, with such outlandish delicacies as ham sandwiches and *cerises à l'eau de vie,* chattering groups of enthusiastic foreign ladies who wore monstrous artificial horse-hair buttocks that could fool the eye of no reasonable man. Recruited by tourist agencies which promised to arrange that they be admitted as guests to the most inaccessible of our aristocratic harems, these impudent unveiled hoydens payed substantial fees, shared by the touts of the tourist industry with their equally impudent hostesses, for the privilege of then swapping clothes all afternoon with their new Turkish friends. The latter were fascinated when they were able to preen themselves in front of a mirror while trying on a Paris hat that looked like a Dutch still life painting of fruit, flowers, vegetables, and dead birds—why never a fish?—or a Viennese *corset brutal* from the world-famous Kärtnerstrasse *atelier* of the firm of *Geschwister Zwieback und Gebrüder Krafft-Ebbing,* while their foreign guests likewise enjoyed seeing themselves wearing veils instead of lorgnettes and feather boas, and ample harem robes instead of wasp-waisted corsets and the absurd prosthetic bottoms that were known in those days as bustles.

Up to a point, all this mascarading was still innocent fun, though it heralded worse to come, I mean the excesses of the present age, when a Turkish gentleman who responds patriotically to his country's call and presents himself for a medical examination before joining our glorious armed forces may suddenly find himself as naked as Adam, our common ancestor, in the Earthly Paradise, but in the presence of a bevy of shameless women who claim to have medical degrees from foreign universities with unpronounceable names, while male film stars run around our streets mysteriously veiled in order to protect their heavily insured complexions from the rays of our relatively mild sun.

Be that all as it may, it came one day to pass, in those innocent days of the reign of Sultan Abdul Hamid, that a French

113

poet reached Istanbul with an assignment, from the editors of *La Vie Parisienne,* to penetrate one of our harems under false pretenses in order to reveal in ribald prose, to his lascivious Parisian readers, the secrets of our traditionally modest family life. Sacrificing his waxed moustache and goatee beard to the cause of what is now known, in our topsy-turvy "unisex" world, as "the free flow of information," this poet dolled himself up, in the privacy of his Pera Palace Hotel apartment, as a rather athletic-looking English maiden lady, all tweeds and tobacco-stained finger tips, and then arranged through the touts who swarm around the offices of the Thomas Cook and Sons travel agency to be included in one of their organized harem parties. This particular group included, in addition to our transvestite poet, among others the wives of two Jewish bankers from Berlin, a Muscovite princess, the late Mrs. Potter Palmer from Chicago, a French *cocotte* traveling as the Comtesse de Mirabelle with an American millionaire from the Barbary Coast, wherever that may be, but who spent all his time in a drunken stupor in his hotel room, and a tight-lipped English suffragette who already planned to distribute leaflets, specially printed in Turkish by an Armenian refugee printer in Manchester, among her unfortunate Moslem sisters, I mean her ignominiously secluded and veiled hostesses.

The French *cocotte,* like many ladies of her profession in that culturally enlightened age, happened to be quite a patroness of the arts and letters, in fact a close friend of Pierre Loti and the original recipient of those *Lettres à une Sphynge* for which Rémy de Gourmont has become justly immortal, and the original model too of the famous representation of a sphinx, half woman and half panther, that earned the Belgian painter Ferdinand Khnopff such immediate celebrity among readers of *The Yellow Book* when he exhibited his masterpiece in London's Grosvenor Gallery. She thus recognized our distinguished French poet at a first glance, in spite of his hairless chin and upper lip and his odd disguise. But she was a woman of some wit, endowed with a curious mind. Smiling enigmatically in the manner that won her the

114

name and reputation of a sphinx, she decided to say nothing and to wait and see.

It thus came to pass that our party of ladies proceeded, in an assortment of arabahs, victorias, barouches, landaus, and other carriages, all the way from the Pera Palace Hotel to a *yali* situated on the shore of the Bosphorus just beyond the Jewish suburb, or Ortaköy, where they were all expected that afternoon as paying guests in one of the more conservative harems of our Ottoman aristocracy. The Turkish ladies of this very proper household had decided but recently, under pressure of their lord and master's heavy gambling debts, to violate their cherished privacy by entertaining, for a considerable fee, only the most carefully selected groups of foreign women.

It was a warm day and the drive was longer than our poet expected. The carriage where he sat was crowded and flea-infested; besides, he was ill at ease in the tight corset to which he was unaccustomed. When the party reached the *yali* of its hostesses, he was already suffering from brief dizzy spells. Later, as the mood of the party became more relaxed, informal, and intimate, the ladies began to swap clothes with delighted squeals. Terrified of being unmasked, our poet remained fully dressed and seated bolt upright on a divan while the beads of sweat trickled down his face and smeared his carefully contrived make-up. The Comtesse de Mirabelle watched him with malicious glee as she performed before his eyes what actually amounted to a striptease. Suddenly, he swooned.

When he came to, the next day, he was surprised by the obsolete pitch of his own voice that rang in his ears like a memory of his almost forgotten and innocent boyhood triumphs as solo singer in a Jesuit College choir. With a shock, our poet realized that he was already an integrated, permanent inmate of this harem into which he had so unwisely ventured. His hostesses, he learned, had kindly rushed to his rescue, when they saw him swoon, and promptly unlaced his corset, revealing a hairy chest beneath the padding that concealed it. To their horror, they then discovered that a man was in their midst. Only one thing could now be done to save their honor. The Chief Eunuch was hastily summoned and instructed to make our poet immediately acceptable as a harem guest.

When he finally recovered from his operation a few weeks later, our poet was entrusted, as a kind of French *mademoiselle,* with the education of the young ladies of the harem, teaching them to recite *par coeur* the poems of Lamartine and of Eugène Manuel. To his editor of *La Vie Parisienne* he explained, in a somewhat evasive letter, that he had fallen in love with the Turkish way of life and would probably never return to his old haunts on the Paris boulevards.

Far from ever violating, for ribald French readers, the secrets of our mysterious Orient, he remained content, in the years that followed, with writing every once in a while a book describing Turkish family life in the most glowing but decorous terms. Several such manuscripts went the round of the Paris publishing houses before finding one that was courageous enough to risk marketing such unusually decent accounts of the secluded life of our harems. Unfortunately, our poet died relatively young, but the few published works of his mature Turkish period are now cherished in France as veritable classics of a rare kind of exoticism that concentrates on the virtues rather than the vices of an alien civilization.

THE ANGEL OF DEATH

The heavy dull-green damask curtains were drawn to exclude the daylight from the hotel room where Haimaki Abulafia, the only child of wealthy parents, lay dying of a mysterious fever. Traveling with his mother and his grandmother on the Orient Express back from Paris to their home in Constantinople, the six-year-old boy first complained of a headache during the first night of their long journey. The next morning, when the blinds of their sleeping car compartment were raised to reveal the snow-clad Swiss landscape, his mother noticed that Haimaki was listless and flushed. From an ample and well-stocked leather dressing case, she unpacked a thermometer and took his temperature. He was only slightly feverish, but she then noted during the day, each time that she took his temperature again, that it was rising steadily. During the ensuing night, the child became delirious for a while, then lapsed into a restless but heavy sleep from which it became increasingly difficult to rouse him. He would awaken from it every once in a while, only to moan and complain briefly of thirst and of pains in his head. When the

117

train reached Vienna in the gray winter dawn, they decided to interrupt their journey and took rooms in one of the big hotels on the Ring.

During the next two days, several of the leading medical celebrities of the Austro-Hungarian capital were summoned in turn to the child's sick bed. Though they disagreed on the cause of the fever, they were all of one opinion, that they had been consulted too late to be at all sure of the results of the treatments or medications that they prescribed. Nor was any one of them ready to face the risk of transporting the dying child from his hotel room to a clinic.

The child's mother and grandmother were in despair. Haimaki no longer seemed even to recognize them, on the rare occasions when he still opened briefly his large, dark, and widely set eyes and reached with a trembling hand for the glass of mineral water that stood on the bedside table, ready to quench his feverish thirst. His father, Behor Abulafia, was on a business trip in distant Iran, purchasing carpets for his stores in Istanbul, Paris, London, and New York. Nobody knew where he could be reached, whether in Teheran, Tabriz, Isfahan, Shiraz, Hamadan, or Meshed. Telegrams had been sent immediately, on his family's arrival in Vienna, to his correspondents in all these cities, but no reply had yet been received. Had he gone further afield, to Herat and Kandahar in wild and turbulent Afghanistan, or perhaps across the border to Bokhara and Samarkand in the Russian Turkestan? One never knew how far his travels might lead him after he reached Teheran, where, in the bazaars, he might hear from one of his agents that some nomad Moslem Prince of the Central Asian steppes was rumored to be short of money and ready to sell a part of his hereditary hoard of rare carpets, or that the notables who administered an almost abandoned mosque, in a once populous city that had now been deserted after many decades of drought, were anxious to sell imperial or royal carpets, donated long ago by a pious Shah or Emir.

Alone and left to their own devices in a strange city, the two

118

women felt utterly helpless. Neither of them spoke or understood any German, but they found that their fluent Levantine French sufficed them for their dealings with the personnel of their hotel and with the Austrian physicians recommended to them by its management. The eminent physician who had just left them was cheerful, like a good actor afflicted with a toothache in a comedy where he knows that he must conceal his personal pain and make his audience laugh. But the sick boy's mother and grandmother were not deceived by the physician's polite display of hope; they sensed that, having failed to prove his medical skill, he had already lost interest in the case, though he promised to return at once, should a change in the patient's condition justify his being summoned again. Now, they were alone in their rooms with the sick boy. Though they refrained from raising their voices lest they disturb him unnecessarily in his comatose sleep, they gave vent to their anxiety in long whispered conversations in Ladino, the language commonly spoken in their homes by the Spanish Jews of the Ottoman Empire.

Was the boy really asleep? Ever since their arrival in Vienna, he had lain there, for three days now and two nights, almost motionless, breathing regularly but never very deep except when, from time to time, he stirred and moaned and reached out a hand that was already too weak to hold the glass of mineral water with which they sought to quench his thirst. He no longer ever uttered a word and had refused for two days to swallow any food. Only the boy's grandmother, old Estella Bembassat, still had hope. Never trusting any physicians, she still believed in her own traditional remedies. Now that all others had failed, her daughter reluctantly and none too hopefully allowed her to have her own way.

Estella Bembassat and her daughter Regina had both been born and raised in Hasköy, a prosperous Sephardic Jewish suburb that overlooks the Golden Horn, beyond the water of which, in the old walled city that had once been capital of the Byzantine Empire, the much older Jewish quarter of Balat, along the waterfront beneath the heights where stood the Greek Orthodox Patriarchate, had become a kind of ghetto, inhabited mainly by the very poor who depended on its community institutions for their livelihood. Though educated in French schools, both women still clung to Ladino as their language as well as to many of the traditional ways of life of the Spanish Jews of the Levant. In spite of the central heating of their Vienna hotel room, for instance, they were now both wearing the long fur-lined house-coats that they generally wore in winter in their home in Con-stantinople, where even the wealthiest are often reduced to such primitive and less effective means of keeping warm, when the cold winds from beyond the Black Sea sweep the domes and minarets of the Imperial city with blizzards as sudden and as cruel as an invasion of bare-backed barbarian horsemen let loose on the Western World by the same unpredictable steppes of Central Asia.

After again consulting her daughter in whispered Ladino, Estella Bembassat now withdrew into the next room and dressed to go out on her errand. When she was ready, she reap-peared briefly, an imposing though somewhat exotic figure. Even when she accompanied her daughter on a journey to Western Europe, she made few concessions to its current fashions in her style of dressing. Beneath her ample black fur coat, which was of a distinctly foreign cut, she was now dressed in the stiff black silks of the older upper-class Spanish-Jewish widows of the Ottoman capital and wore, instead of a hat, a black veil that was bound around her head and face and fell over her shoul-ders so that she looked almost like a Catholic nun. As if to avoid being mistaken for a nun, she held conspicuously in her one ungloved hand a Moslem rosary of dark yellow-brown amber beads which she told nervously, concentrating all her anxiety in this one harmless tic so as to be free to act all the more deci-sively and efficiently in every other respect.

After taking leave of her daughter, she went downstairs and consulted briefly the hotel porter in French. Having ascertained her way from him, she asked for a cab. When the doorman helped her into the horse-drawn cab that he hailed for her, its surprised driver could scarcely believe his ears as she gave him, in her heavy foreign accent, an address in Vienna's very poorest Jewish quarter, situated in the depths of Leopoldstadt, beyond the Danube Canal. Fares picked up at this elegant hotel, he mused, might well have been born in such a lowly ghetto, but rarely went back there, even on brief visits, especially on as cruel a winter afternoon as this.

Low gray clouds had been hanging all day over Vienna, threatening it with a blizzard. When Estella Bembassat set forth on her errand, the snow was just beginning to fall on the sidewalks of the almost deserted Ring. When the cab reached the corner by the Opera where the Kärntnerstrasse begins, a great gust of wind rising toward them from the open spaces of the Karlplatz enveloped them in a cloud of snow, like a sandstorm in a desert. As the blizzard invaded the Kärntnerstrasse and swept up toward the Stefanskirche, the few shoppers who were still on the sidewalks hastily sought refuge in doorways or in the more sheltered side streets.

The snow was already falling thick on the deserted sidewalks of the Ring when Estella Bembassat returned two hours later to her hotel, now accompanied by an ancient Rabbi whose appearance and dress suggested that he belonged to a strange community of Balkan Jews from Bosnia or from some other exotic province of the southern marches of the Austro-Hungarian Empire. Two younger acolytes followed them now in a second cab; their appearance and dress were as strange as their Master's. As they all four stepped out of their cabs onto the sidewalk where the snow reflected the light of the streetlamps so that the Ring now seemed, in the evening, more bright and less gray than it had been by daylight, their darkly clad figures stood out sharply against their background and might easily have called to mind some macabre old tale of guests of ill omen who came to a wedding dressed as if for a funeral.

The two younger men unloaded from their cab a large Turkish-style brass *mangal,* or brasero, for heating a room with glowing charcoal embers, then also two closed wicker baskets. From

121

the sounds that escaped from one of the baskets, it appeared to contain a restless live bird. Following Estella Bembassat with their loads into the entrance hall of the hotel where their appearance attracted considerable attention, they took the elevator and soon found themselves in the sick child's room.

In the middle of the room, behind drawn curtains, the two young acolytes set up the brass *mangal,* filled it with charcoal from one of the baskets, then lit a fire in it, taking the necessary precautions to avoid filling the room with noxious fumes. The old Rabbi had meanwhile drawn a compass from the pocket of his caftan and consulted it to make sure that he would be facing east when he would begin, as soon as everything was ready, to invoke in prayer the aid of the Lord. Before praying, the Rabbi warned the two women that, whatever he now did, they must never pronounce again Haimaki's given name in the boy's presence. As his acolytes cast incense and various herbs or powders in the fire, the Rabbi began to pray beneath his shawl while the room was gradually filled with swirling and powerfully scented fumes.

When the room was as full of these fumes as one of those hallowed caves of antiquity where the volcanic vapors caused a Sybil's oracular trances, the acolytes opened the second basket and took out of it a live black cock that flapped its wings wildly as it sought to escape from their grasp. Holding the doomed cock upside down by its feet so that the blood rushed to its head and soon produced a stupor that reduced its struggles to inertia, the older acolyte approached the Rabbi who, as soon as he had completed his prayers, seized the bird in his left hand while the other acolyte handed him a sharp knife that he now held in his right hand as he approached the sick boy's bed.

The death rattle could already be heard in Haimaki's throat as the Rabbi raised the knife above his head and, in Ladino, called upon the boy in a loud and imperative tone, urging him to forget his given name and renaming him now with the secret name of the doomed cock, since all things created have a name in the mind of their Creator. Then the Rabbi solemnly gave the cock the name of the dying boy and, summoning the Angel of

122

Death to come and fetch his prey, plunged the knife in the cock's throat, letting its blood flow abundantly over the boy's head, where it soon soaked into his tangled dark hair that was already matted with feverish sweat. The boy's mother uttered a cry of horror, but his grandmother seemed to be content and confident.

A few minutes later, as the Rabbi and his acolytes took their leave, the boy was already breathing more normally and appeared to be sleeping quite peacefully. For three days, the clotted blood of the cock was left to dry on the boy's head, like a poultice that covered his hair. On the fourth day, he complained only of weakness and wished to eat. A Viennese doctor who had previously been consulted in vain and never been summoned again but, prompted by mere professional curiosity, now called to find out how his former patient fared, had to admit that the child seemed to have fully recovered from his almost fatal fever.

But the Angel of Death, though cheated in Vienna, took his revenge elsewhere. The Rabbi had indeed warned the two women that the boy must henceforth be addressed always by his new name, and that his former given name should never be uttered again in his presence. But the boy's father, in distant Kabul, knew nothing of this warning. At last, he had received there, forwarded from Teheran, one of his wife's urgent messages from Vienna. At once, he wrote her a letter, announcing his immediate return and expressing the pious hope that, with God's will, Haimaki might already be out of danger. In his letter to his wife, he enclosed a brief note addressed directly to his son: "*Haimaki, mi querido hijico, verdadero pasha de tu padre. . . .*" When he went out to post this letter, Behor Abulafia found himself caught in one of the disturbances that so frequently occurred in those times in the bazaars of Afghanistan, a nation torn by civil strife while Russian and British agents struggled to bring it within their respective spheres of influence. Before posting his letter, Behor Abulafia was stabbed to death by one of the followers of a fanatical *mullah,* on the day that he had unwittingly addressed his son in writing by his name that was now forbidden.

123

IV

THE ETERNAL AND
UBIQUITOUS CITY

A MAN OF EDUCATION AND CULTURE

My grandfather first drifted out west to San Francisco long before the great Earthquake and the Fire and very nearly decided to settle there for good rather than in Boston. The hills of downtown San Francisco reminded him of Pera in his native Istanbul; the views of the Bay suggested to him those of the Golden Horn and the Bosphorus; the Italian restaurants along Fishermen's Wharf had not yet become an internationally famous tourist attraction and were still as unpretentious, in their surprisingly Southern European informality, as the Greek fishing villages that had been his boyhood haunts along the Bosphorus, near Therapia or Büyük Dere. Even the timber architecture of old San Francisco reminded him of the older quarters of Istanbul as he had known them in his boyhood, with the elaborate bow windows of the houses from which the Californian women could peer from behind their curtains at whatever might be happening in the street, like the wives and daughters of a middle-class Turkish home from their harem in a nineteenth-century timber mansion decorated with the gingerbread ornaments for which the Laz shipbuilders and carpenters of the Black Sea coast of Northern Anatolia were once famous in the Ottoman capital and which the German carpenters of Northern California seemed to emulate. Nor was my grandfather the only native of the Turkish capital to feel attracted in this manner to San Francisco, which has now become the home of an important colony of Armenian and Greek immigrants from Istanbul and its suburbs along the coasts of the Bosphorus and the Sea of Marmara. Those to whom Istanbul has once been home are always and everywhere haunted by memories of its beauty. But in San Francisco, everything conspires to remind them even more poignantly of their native city.

A Turkish-born Armenian American, Dick Sarkissian already enjoyed in San Francisco a local reputation as a cook and restaurant owner. He had prospered by catering to customers who appreciate Oriental food prepared *neat,* without any American trimmings and with no concessions to the tastes, fads, and fashions of his new Californian home. His yogurt, for instance, was home-made, totally unlike the factory-made product sold under the same name in American supermarkets. The mutton for his shish kebabs was purchased from San Francisco's best *kosher* butcher, because Jews slaughter their animals in the same manner as the Moslem Turks, so that their meat has been drained of blood and is less red than that of other butchers. One of the only concessions that Dikran Sarkissian made to Americanization seemed to be to allow the customers of "The Golden Horn" to call him Dick instead of Dikran, the name of so many great Armenian kings of antiquity whom Greek and Roman historians called Tigranes.

During the year that I taught as a guest at San Francisco State College, I became one of Dick's regular customers. If I came early or late, at an hour when "The Golden Horn" was not too crowded, he would sit at my table to reminisce with me, over Turkish coffee or *raki* served on the house, about his boyhood spent, before the great Armenian massacres at the end of the First World War, on the Asian shore in Üsküdar, across the

128

Bosphorus from Istanbul. At the end of my year in San Francisco, when I decided to return to Paris via the Far East and, on my way, to stop in Istanbul too, I went to Dick's restaurant, one Monday evening when we would not be disturbed by too many other customers, to discuss my plans with him.

It was then that Dick asked me to look up in Istanbul one of his relatives, a Turkish Armenian medical student to whom he had been sending, for many years, a small monthly allowance in order to help him complete his studies. Dick gave me the student's name, Garabed Varjian, and his postal address; I immediately assumed that I would be meeting a man of about thirty, at most.

I experienced some difficulty in locating Garabed Varjian in Istanbul. Dick Sarkissian had indicated to me only the *poste restante* in Beyoglu where his student relative collected his mail. In addition, Dick could remember, from a brief trip made to Turkey shortly after the Second World War, that Garabed Varjian then lived in a narrow street off Beyoglu, to the left as one walked downhill to the Galata Sarai high school, in fact almost behind the school and in a small apartment house situated opposite the entrance to a neighborhood *hamam,* or Turkish bath.

I wrote to Garabed Varjian shortly after my arrival in Istanbul, but received no reply. I found moreover a letter from Dick Sarkissian awaiting me at my hotel: he wished me to find out why, in spite of the financial aid received from America for more than fifteen years, Garabed Varjian had not yet obtained his medical degree. Was he a victim of anti-Armenian discrimination whenever he came up for his exams at the Turkish University? If this was the case, might it not be wiser for him to emigrate and complete his medical studies abroad? Would I be kind enough to discuss all this with Garabed Varjian and report my findings back to Dick in San Francisco? Dick's letter convinced me that I should make an effort to see his relative before returning to America, if only to avoid unnecessary embarrassment should I ever find myself dining again in San Francisco at "The Golden Horn."

129

One afternoon I therefore set out to locate Varjian in his backstreet apartment off Beyoglu, since I also had some shopping to do in that section of the city. After attending to my own errands, I turned off Beyoglu's main street to the left, up the last narrow street that branches off before one reaches the monumental marble and ironwork gates of the Galata Sarai high school. I was fortunate: the narrow street which I had thus chosen turned suddenly to the left again so as to join the end of the last street that likewise branched off Beyoglu. Almost opposite where the two streets met, I found indeed a small neighborhood Turkish bath and then began to look for the apartment house where Garabed Varjian might still live.

There were only three apartment houses that answered Dick's description of the one where his relative lived. The other houses in the block opposite the Turkish bath, between the bend in the street that led me there and the entrance to the other narrow street that led back to Beyoglu, were a dependency of a nearby Greek secondary school for girls and an annex of the Italian Consulate. All five buildings were equally shabby in this rundown Christian ghetto now occupied by a residue of the former population of nineteenth-century Beyoglu, which had been Istanbul's more prosperous European section, once inhabited mainly by Christians and Jews.

Relying on my very limited Turkish, I approached the *kapuju,* or doorman, of the first of these three apartment houses, interrupting his job of salvaging whatever valuables he might still find in the building's overflowing garbage cans. He was very dark and sharp-featured but happened, in spite of his typically Turkish or Kurdish appearance, to be a Greek, which made it all the more easy for me to obtain information from him, since I happen to speak Greek more fluently than Turkish. Nor was I surprised that he should be a Greek, in this backstreet ghetto of impecunious formerly middle-class Greeks, Armenians, and Levantine Catholics who had all seen better days and now eked out a precarious livelihood in an increasingly unfriendly Turkish economy, always fearing new outbursts of mob violence inspired by the political tensions in Cyprus, so that Christian tenants might no longer feel safe in a building kept by a presumably hostile Turkish doorman.

Seeing that I spoke Greek, the doorman proved to be helpful. Garabed Varjian, he told me, did not happen to live in his building, but might well be a tenant in one of the other two apartment houses. After questioning in vain his colleague of the first of these, he found out from the doorman of the second that Garabed Varjian had been living there for many years, on the very top floor.

The entrance and staircase of this apartment house were even shabbier than those of the two others. I toiled up five flights of a narrow, steep, and dark staircase, past doors off which the paint had peeled many years ago, past tiny windows with broken panes, all opening onto a diminutive and filthy yard or ventilation shaft, cluttered at the bottom with a modern kitchen midden's deposits of rotting garbage and old newspapers. Through these dark windows, a ghastly sour smell invaded the staircase, a compound of the exhalations of the refuse decomposing at the bottom of the shaft and of the vapors escaping into it from the kitchens and toilets of the various tenants. When I reached the third floor, I found more light in the staircase and less stink: the house next door, where the Italian Consulate had its annex, had only two upper floors, so that the ventilation shaft above its roof was now open on one side, letting in more light and air. On the top floor, the staircase window had no panes at all. They had been replaced with burlap, which had slowly rotted, so that the rain could then come in, repeatedly flooding the floor until its boards too began to rot. In addition, brown stains in the plaster of the ceiling revealed that the roof above the top landing also leaked whenever it rained.

Opposite the stairs, I found only one door, whereas on all the other landings I had seen the doors of two apartments. I pressed the doorbell. There was no reply. Then it occurred to me that I had heard no bell ring, so I knocked on the door. I soon heard a shuffling behind the door, then a clanging of iron bars being removed as a voice asked me in Turkish who I was. Finally, when I briefly explained my errand, the door was opened and I found myself facing an elderly man, almost bald but with sparse gray hair on the back and the sides of his head. He was pasty-faced and wore a filthy tattered bathrobe or dressing gown. The slippers on his feet were like those that one might find emerging from a garbage pail standing by the doorway of a tenement. Behind him I could detect, in the semidarkness, a room of inde-scribable poverty and squalor.

"Mr. Varjian?" I inquired. He nodded assent, and it ocurred to me that he must be the medical student's father. I explained in greater detail the nature of my errand, apologizing for dis-turbing him during the siesta hour and asking him whether his son was at home. He replied that he had no son: he was Gara-bed Varjian, the student of medicine. Ushering me into the flat, he opened a door that led beyond the first room, a kind of kitchen scullery where every tap or pipe seemed to leak as if plumbers had long become extinct in Turkey, into a penthouse veranda with wooden partitions up to the height of a man's waist, above which windows, most of them filthy or with broken panes held together by paper and glue, allowed one to enjoy, if one was in the right mood, an admirable view over the rooftops of lower Pera and Tophane, across the Bosphorus and as far as the hills of the Asiatic coast. I realized at once that this wooden veranda was no real apartment but the building's former roof-top laundry, having originally been used by the tenants to hang their linen to dry when it was raining outside. The first room, with all its leaking pipes and taps and its wealth of vats like kitchen sinks which I had seen in semidarkness, had been the actual laundry.

The whole apartment was summarily but very oddly fur-nished. On the veranda's floor, in a far corner, lay a sorely mis-used mattress, its bedding unmade, the torn and grayish sheets bundled together with equally torn and colorless blankets. A few rickety chairs were distributed at random. On one pre-carious table, a spirit lamp, with a few tired and unsavory-

132

looking saucepans hanging from rusty nails in the wall above it, constituted the summary kitchen of an apparently slovenly bachelor who could scarcely be a gourmet. Another precarious table, somewhat larger, had once been used as a desk, if the ink-stains on the wooden top had any meaning. It was now cluttered with a few cracked and unwashed dishes, cups, and glasses that lay there beneath the spreading fronds of a couple of irregularly watered and anemic-looking potted plants. In the middle of all this, like a refugee Russian Princess who had sunk to the lower depths of a drab Paris suburb where former Tsarist officers live and find employment as cab drivers for nearby garages, a very battered but once elegant rococo lady's dressing table of about 1900 stood with its three cracked mirrors that were held together by damaged hinges as precariously as the panels of a triptych above the altar of an abandoned and desecrated chapel. All around, the floor of the veranda was littered with piles of old newspapers, old cartons filled with accumulated and unidentifiable odds and ends, empty bottles and jars of every shape and size, scattered books that looked even more tired and dusty than those uninviting odd volumes of the complete works of Oliver Wendell Holmes or Sir Walter Scott that one sometimes finds offered for sale, but with so little conviction that they can almost more easily be stolen, on a sidewalk stand outside a desperately poor secondhand furniture shop in a slum.

Garabed Varjian motioned me toward the best of his three rickety chairs. In faltering and lisping French, he launched into an apologetic rigmarole that became increasingly vague and querulous. In this benighted country, he tried to explain to me, it was impossible for a Christian to obtain a medical degree without political pull, which would cost money in bribes and *bakshish*. Were he able to pass his examinations at the Turkish University in spite of his being a Christian, it was still doubtful whether, as an Armenian, he would ever be admitted as an intern in a Turkish hospital or subsequently be able to establish himself in private practice in Istanbul, which is already over-crowded with Armenian doctors who require a special permit to

133

reside elsewhere in Turkey. As I listened to his defeatist arguments, I became increasingly skeptical till I interrupted him to point out that, in the more prosperous neighborhood of Taksim, I had observed, by the doors of many obviously expensive apartment houses, the signs of physicians whose names appeared to be Armenian. Besides, I had already met an Armenian who, having completed his medical studies at Istanbul University, had been able to obtain admission as an intern to the Armenian Hospital.

Garabed Varjian agreed that such privileged cases existed, but all these more successful Armenians had powerful family connections within the Armenian community or wealthy parents or both, whereas he had nobody in Turkey to help or encourage him in his studies. I then reminded him of the bounties of his American relative, which only made him smile apologetically as he fluttered a pudgy gray-fleshed hand in a gesture of weary deprecation. After a few more minutes of hopelessly desultory conversation that soon degenerated into an exchange of polite banalities, I rose from my rickety chair and took my leave. That same evening, I wrote to his cousin in San Francisco, limiting my report to a brief paragraph stating that I had found Garabed Varjian very discouraged about his chances of ever being admitted in Turkey to the medical profession.

Having thus done my duty, I no longer intended to see Garabed Varjian again, since I knew of less depressing and more profitable ways of spending my spare time in Istanbul, one of the world's most excitingly many-sided cities, where every day the tourist can visit another enchanting monument or discover another breathtakingly beautiful view of the city or of its environs.

A couple of weeks later, however, I found myself again in his neighborhood, looking for a secondhand bookshop where I had been told that I might still find with luck, at reasonable prices, a few loose pages of old Turkish manuscripts containing hand-illuminated miniatures. When I finally found the shop and entered it, I recognized Varjian there, engaged in an argument

134

with the owner, who appeared to be offering him a couple of banknotes for a book with which Varjian indignantly refused to part at this price. Varjian had not yet seen me and was holding the book open in his hand, pointing excitedly at a page which appeared to be illustrated. Every deal in Istanbul is accompanied by some measure of excited haggling and bargaining about the price. But Varjian, as soon as he caught sight of me and recognized me, closed the book hurriedly, greeted me with a nervous smile, and left the shop without more ado, as if in guilty flight.

One evening, a few days later, I was coming out of a movie-house in a side street of Beyoglu, when I again saw Varjian. This time, he was being insulted vigorously in Turkish by two very rough and heavily-built young workmen who looked like recent immigrants to Istanbul from some Anatolian village. A crowd was already gathering around them, many of the men laughing cynically or commenting on the altercation with quips and taunts of their own. My limited knowledge of Turkish did not permit me to understand most of the argument, in the course of which a great deal of abuse, of slang, and of Anatolian dialect appeared to be used.

Varjian was answering his tormentors only intermittently, in a terrified and shrill voice, reminding me of the batlike twitter of Homeric ghosts. Pale with fear, he seemed almost featureless, with only his eyes and mouth emerging from the wrinkled bloodless mass of his face that appeared roughly molded in a mass of grayish dough over which his facial expression only hovered, suggesting mortified but indignant innocence. When he caught sight of me in the crowd, he seemed for a while to be even more embarrassed than on the occasion of our last meeting in the bookshop. But as the verbal vehemence of his persecutors increased, now accompanied also by gestured threats of physical violence, he hesitated briefly, then rushed toward me as if seeking protection, clutched my arm, and pushed me through the crowd to the door of a nearby restaurant where we found sanctuary together.

Through the glass door we could still see the two young roughnecks watching us, like ferocious fish through the glass front of an aquarium, as the crowd slowly dispersed. Varjian had meanwhile collapsed in a chair and breathlessly ordered two glasses of tea. As he mopped with a filthy rag of a handkerchief the sweat that trickled in heavy drops from his wrinkled brow, he looked at me across the marble-topped table at which we were seated and exclaimed in a voice that was almost a whimper: "This nation of barbarians! Will they never learn to respect a man of education and culture?"

Through the glass door to which he turned his back, I could see beyond him his two persecutors, still threatening us with clenched fists and ferocious grimaces. Seeing me quite unperturbed, one of them suddenly grinned almost good-naturedly. He then shrugged his shoulders and spoke a few words to his companion, after which they turned and began to walk off, with their fists thrust deep in their pockets and their broad backs swaying as if to suggest the threat of idle muscular strength that could all too easily explode in acts of violence. The one who had grinned turned round, however, to grin again and greet me with his right hand now raised in a frankly friendly gesture before they both disappeared around a bend of the street.

I was puzzled, but preferred not to question Varjian about the whole incident, knowing that I could expect from him only evasive and vague explanations. He was obviously relieved to see it all end so soon and so peacefully. Had I saved him from the kind of mob violence that had once led in these very streets to Armenian massacres? We sat there in silence, sipping our tea. A few minutes later, Varjian excused himself hesitantly, after fumbling in his pockets, for being unable to pay for our two glasses of tea. I did my best to put him at his ease, after which he thanked me profusely for my help and hospitality, explained that he was tired and not feeling too well, then rose from his chair and hastened away.

By now, I was frankly intrigued by the mysteries of this nondescript little man's life. During the next few days, however, I found no time to pursue the investigation that I planned. Then, one afternoon, I called on him again in his sordid penthouse.

This time, when he opened the door, I heard no preliminary clanking of iron bars. Presumably, he was not feeling so insecure today that he felt the need to barricade himself in his home. But he was even more embarrassed than on our two previous meetings when he now opened his door and recognized me, even hesitating to let me into the flat, so that I almost forced my way past him, chattering pleasantly to conceal the apparent rudeness of my intrusion as he followed me past the dripping taps and pipes of the laundry vats to the veranda beyond.

When I reached the veranda, I understood at once why my presence, as a friend of his American relative and benefactor, now posed problems. Varjian happened to be entertaining in his home a few guests of a truly surprising nature: the two young men whom I had found insulting and threatening him in the street a couple of days earlier and two older men, both of Varjian's age but less shabby in dress and physical appearance. One of these, a fat Levantine, was a flagrant homosexual whose sparse hair was brightly dyed with henna and whose flabby cheeks were profusely powdered, so that his naturally florid complexion was revealed in mauve and blue stains like bruises barely concealed beneath make-up that was of far too milky a hue. The other, a prim and restless man whose expressions and gestures were those of an English spinster, perhaps a governess, of the Edwardian era, turned out subsequently to be a somewhat timorous Swiss tourist. I seemed to have interrupted their conversation just as the fat Levantine was showing the two boys some pictures in an open book. Before he had time to close and conceal it, I snatched it from his hands, almost as if I were a policeman raiding this strange meeting place, and began to examine the drawings that embellished it.

As I turned its pages, I discovered that it was an old French textbook of anatomy, innocuous enough in its outer appearance. But someone had pasted into it, on alternate pages, an extraordinary collection of obscene and hair-raisingly sadistic drawings,

137

all representing Turkish soldiers and sailors, naked but still wearing their boots, caps, and belts and carrying various weapons as they tortured and raped equally naked young boys and girls.

The fat was now in the fire and Varjian realized that I fully understood what was afoot, though my expression revealed amused surprise rather than disapproval or horror. Again, he fluttered a deprecating hand as he smiled nervously and reached for the book, taking it away from me: "I see you're a man of education and culture. One has to earn a living somehow. Would you care to look at some more of my drawings?"

From a folder, Varjian began to produce a series of larger and more detailed loose-leaf drawings, all of them like caricatural memories of a massacre, some of them even representing bloodthirsty ruffians still abusing the decapitated or otherwise mutilated corpses of their young victims in a veritable orgy of sadistic necrophilia. Bored after glancing at a good dozen of these weird fantasies, I raised my eyes from the one that he was showing me. The five other occupants of the veranda were staring at me curiously. My eyes happened to meet those of the young Anatolian villager who had grinned at me in so surprisingly friendly a manner before turning his back on us and going away when we had first met, on the occasion of Varjian's altercation with him and his companion a few days earlier. Again, he smiled, revealing his strong white teeth and healthily pink gums that contrasted with his swarthy complexion and thin black mustache. Then he laughed, looked at me questioningly with bright and fearless eyes, frowned a while in deep thought, finally blurted out, in the rudimentary English of a waterfront tout: "You American? Want to meet nice girl?"

I apologized to Varjian and his guests for my intrusion and prepared to leave. Varjian accompanied me back to the door. As I began descending the stairs, I didn't hear him close it behind me. Suddenly, I heard a heavy clatter of hobnailed boots behind me and was heartily slapped on the back. The two Anatolian boys had followed me, both laughing like children escap-

138

ing after playing some prank. When we reached the street, they insisted that I buy them a drink in a neighboring tavern. In a mixture of waterfront English and equally rudimentary and ungrammatical Turkish, we conversed over our beers as they both explained to me, aiding themselves with obscene gestures when I failed to understand their Turkish slang, how Varjian had once recruited them in the street to procure them for his wealthier friends, but had subsequently failed on several occasions to pass on to them the full sum of money that he led them to expect and probably collected for them from their customers.

After the first round of beers, they decided to treat me in turn to a second. Later, I paid a third round and bought them a meal too. During the next few hours, they proved to be excellent company, grateful for my hospitality, careful not to abuse it, but anxious too to show me all the low haunts, the backstreet taverns and brothels of the waterfront neighborhoods of Karaköy and Tophane. Somehow, I felt quite safe in their company. They behaved indeed as if I had just saved them from some threat, much as I had likewise saved Varjian from them a few nights earlier. When we parted, I slipped a folded banknote into the hand of the one who had first revealed to me his friendly feelings. They both seemed to be overwhelmed with gratitude. A couple of minutes later, I heard someone running behind me. The one who had always proved most friendly was again beside me. He had bought a red rose from a street vendor and now carefully inserted it in the buttonhole of my lapel. A blush suffused his swarthy face as he smiled, grasped my shoulders with both hands, hugged me and kissed me on both cheeks, calling me *kardeshim,* meaning "my brother," before he turned away and ran off, bashful as a child.

THE GHOST WITH AN AMERICAN PASSPORT

In some of the older and less commercial streets of the downtown area of Fresno, a stranger may still be surprised to find a few dilapidated houses built in a style of architecture which is neither that of the usual turn-of-the-century "gingerbread" timber homes of Northern California, nor the pseudo-Spanish "mission" style which gradually superseded it but had once been indigenous, in a more functional and less coyly picturesque version, to much of Southern California. Instead, these houses in Fresno have an unmistakably Near Eastern aspect, reminding one of the homes in any Turkish city of some sixty years ago. They have heavily shuttered projecting bay windows, like those of a middle-class Moslem harem, and oddly shaped roofs that extend much further over the sidewalk than those of most other Californian houses, as if to protect their windows from the glare of the sun.

Twenty years ago, these Turkish-style houses were a distinctive feature of some residential sections of Fresno, where they had once been far more numerous. In the postwar building boom that swept over the city after 1945 as over the rest of California, all but the last few of these old houses have been demolished to make room for more modern and commercial real estate developments. But they should perhaps have been preserved as historical monuments, illustrating the cultural and social history of Fresno, which owes much of its prosperity to the industry of its important Armenian community. Escaping from Turkey at the time of the great massacres, much as Jews also escaped in the same decades to America from the pogroms of Tsarist Russia, these Armenians, as soon as they had made enough money in Fresno, felt themselves inspired to build homes there in the architectural style to which they had been accustomed in their fatherland, perhaps because they felt less alien in the Californian climate and landscape than other Armenian refugees who settled and prospered elsewhere in America. A whole section of Fresno thus came to be built almost exclusively in this Turkish style of architecture, each one of its homes swarming with Armenian grandmothers, grandfathers, great-uncles, and great-aunts who looked, behaved, and spoke exactly as if in a story by William Saroyan. On the sidewalks of downtown Fresno, elderly Armenians indeed continued for many years to amble or shuffle along, absent-mindedly telling their amber worry beads exactly as if they were wandering through the alleys of a covered Turkish bazaar.

Born in one of these Turkish-style houses of Fresno, Aram Haruntunian was a young third-generation Californian Armenian when he was drafted into the United States Air Force and sent on overseas duty to a base in Adana, in Southeastern Turkey. Dark haired, he had the aquiline profile that distinguished his father and grandfather. His heavy black eyebrows, as in a Persian miniature, were almost joined above the ridge of his nose. In spite of his American schooling, he still looked typically Armenian, if not Kurdish or Persian. From his grandparents, he had heard much of their native land, of which they cherished somewhat ambivalent memories, both of the easy life that they had once led there in Konya and Istanbul and of the horrors from which they had almost miraculously escaped when the Armenian massacres swept across Turkey like a raging storm. Again and again, Aram had listened to his grandfather, old George Haruntunian, known in Armenian as Kevork, explaining how he had been born a wealthy merchant's son in Konya, where their family supplied windowpanes and mirrors to the whole province before moving to Istanbul, to prosper there in the same business when the city's new European quarters in Pera were the scene of a building boom during the latter quarter of the nineteenth century. "In Psamatia, near the big Armenian church in the old city," Aram's grandfather boasted, "I owned my own house. It was a fine new house, I had it built in a new street, Kutulmusoglu Sokak, and that's why I then built another one here exactly like it."

Often, the old man wondered what might have become of his old home in Psamatia, on the heights of Old Istanbul that overlook Langna, which had once been a Byzantine harbor on the shore of the Sea of Marmara. He had fled from it with his family in the middle of the night, having been warned by a faithful Turkish apprentice of the approaching mob. Abandoning his home with all that it contained, he had escaped the next day to Egypt, with other wealthy Armenian merchants, on a ship which Old Man Tokatleyan, the owner of Istanbul's most modern hotel, had somehow managed to charter through the *Compagnie Internationale des Wagons-lits,* which was then building its own rival hotel a few blocks away, the Pera Palace. It had been a shipload of terrified millionaires and their families; one of them, a young man who happened to be a poor relative of a wealthy carpet merchant, was Calouste Gulbenkian, who later became one of the world's wealthiest men, a now legendary oil magnate.

Before leaving for Turkey on overseas duty, Aram promised his grandfather that he would visit Istanbul on one of his leaves from his air base in Adana, and would try to find the house and send back to Fresno, if he could, a photograph of it. After spending a couple of months near Adana, Aram Haruntunian was at last able to apply for a few days' leave in order to visit

142

Istanbul. Having booked a room in a *turistik* hotel in the more modern or European section of the former Turkish capital, he found the porter there of little assistance in advising him how to locate in distant Psamatia the modest street, Kutulmusoglu Sokak, where his grandfather's house might still be standing. Kutulmusoglu Sokak was indeed listed in no guidebook of Istanbul and marked on no map of the city. After many fruitless enquiries, Aram decided to take a cab to Psamatia and fend there for himself.

Leaving his cab in front of the big Armenian Church, Aram went into a nearby tea house to ask in Armenian whether anybody could direct him from there to Kutulmusoglu Sokak. Here too, he made little progress. A toothless old woman could indeed remember that there had once been such a street in this neighborhood in her childhood, but all streets in Psamatia had been renamed after heroes of Turkish national liberation since Kemal Ataturk had reorganized the shattered remains of the former Ottoman Empire as a modern republic. Try as she might, she couldn't for the life of her remember which street near here had been Kutulmusoglu Sokak, though she seemed to think that one of her nieces had been engaged to a young tailor who lived there before they married and emigrated to Lebanon. Did Aram come from Lebanon? Perhaps he had known her niece there. . . .

After much gossip of this kind, Aram finally found, in a grocery store, a sprightly old man who could well remember which street had once been Kutulmusoglu Sokak. How could he fail to remember it? In his boyhood, it had become for a while, shortly after the massacres, a street of houses of ill fame, hastily set up in the abandoned homes of wealthy Armenians who had fled. He laughed lustily as he now remembered some of the good times he had had as a boy in Kutulmusoglu Sokak. In one of the houses, there had even been a Sudanese Negress who was famous in the neighborhood as a sorceress, selling love charms to the jealous wives of her customers. She had been no fool. . . .

When Aram finally found Redjep Shaoush Sokak, as it was

143

now called, he discovered a quiet street that had obviously been, many years ago, a prosperous residential neighborhood, before it had fallen upon evil days from which it never recovered. It was not very long, with only a dozen houses on each side. Some of the houses stood in ruins, utterly abandoned, other still appeared to be inhabited, though they were all in various stages of disrepair. One of the more solidly built inhabited houses, toward the middle of the block on Aram's left, might well have been the home that his grandfather had so often described; it was almost exactly like their old home in Fresno, but a bit older and more run down, in fact already almost a ruin. Its roof had caved in over half of the upper story, which was now only partly occupied, where the roof was precariously patched together with old and rusting pieces of tin that looked as if they might have been taken from discarded containers of some kind. Most of the windows of the house no longer had any glass panes. Some were boarded with rotting wood, others were equipped with jute sacking or pieces of board from old cartons as a substitute for panes.

Aram stood in front of the house, in the middle of the street, staring at the house and wondering whether he dare take a picture of it to send to his grandfather. Might it not be kinder to let the old man continue cherishing his old illusions, rather than to shatter them by confronting them with the realities of the present? Suddenly, the door of the house was opened by a very old woman who stood there and stared at Aram in speechless wonder, wide-eyed and open-mouthed, till she uttered a scream and scampered down the street, shouting repeatedly at the top of her voice: *"Djamdji burda,* the glazier is back again!"

Still screaming, she disappeared around the corner, but returned a few minutes later accompanied by a small group of very old people, who gathered in a circle around Aram, staring at him incredulously. Finally, one of them plucked up enough courage to approach him, to feel his arm as if to see that he was real and no apparition, and to exclaim: "Why do you have to dress like an American tourist, Kevork Effendim, to come back

144

and haunt your old home? Are you afraid we might kill you because we have been living all these years in your house without paying you any rent? Ever since the night you fled, we have tried to look after it for you. When the mob came, we were already there and they found only Turks living in it. But now we're too old and too poor to look after it properly. Anyhow, what use can an old house now be to a ghost? Only a ghost can live over sixty years like you, Kevork Effendim, without showing any sign of aging. . . ."

To prove that he was not his own living grandfather's ghost, Aram then produced his American passport. The occupants of the house were his grandfather's former Turkish apprentice and his family. A few days later, Aram sent his grandfather a photograph of the house, together with one of himself drinking coffee with the old people in the garden behind the house, where the fruit trees that George Haruntunian had once planted had prospered and were now in blossom.

A NIGHT OF LOVE

It was snowing fitfully and ineffectually in Beyoglu, which had once been the prosperous European section of Ottoman Istanbul. The heavy and soft flakes melted in the air and failed to form white lawns on the dark sidewalks which were flooded instead with slush. Depressing enough in such weather by daylight, Istanbul's main commercial thoroughfare tonight seemed desperately sordid. Its cautious Greek and Armenian jewelers, whose showcases display during shopping hours the only examples of splendid luxury in this formerly elegant neighborhood now slowly become gray with age and already beginning to look almost like a slum, had removed their precious wares, as usual, from their grilled and unlit windows, which were now as dark and sightless as the eyes of a blind beggar.

On leave from his American air base in Southeastern Anatolia, Captain Stanton Cunliffe tottered hesitantly down the street, looking like a rare exotic leaf driven by the cold wind, in fact an inappropriately well-dressed figure in these otherwise desolate few blocks that lead beyond Beyoglu's cheaper striptease night clubs to the *Tunel* underground cable-car connection with the downtown waterfront.

It was a weekday, already late, close on midnight. The street was almost empty of traffic, and Captain Stanton Cunliffe attracted only the attention of those few passers-by who were still out for no good purpose, touts for night clubs and brothels or peddlers hawking hashish, pornographic photographs, or contraband imports from bar to bar. Some of them turned back to stare at him with the eager look of a scavenger bird, but the Captain went his way without even glancing at them, so that those who might have hoped to attract his attention soon lost interest in him and hurried on their mysterious nocturnal pursuit of ever-elusive profits.

The Captain was tall, slim, broad-shouldered, and quite conspicuous in this neighborhood and at this hour of the night. The ample turned-up collar of his expensive beige camel's hair overcoat concealed the lower part of his face, the rest of which remained in the shadow of the brim of his felt hat, pitched forward on his forehead to protect his eyes from the falling snow. Like a knight in armor, he peered forth, from between the brim of his hat and his upturned collar, as if through the narrow slit visor of a steel helmet. His hands were thrust deep into his overcoat pockets, beneath the belt that he wore tightly pulled round his slim waist. Had they been endowed with self-expression, his fine handmade English suede shoes might have protested loudly against being dragged as now through such an inferno of mud and slush.

Suddenly, the Captain stopped, looked around carefully as if seeking a landmark, made up his mind, and turned off Beyoglu to the right, up a narrow and dark alley that looked as if it had been specially designed as a set for a cutthroat film about low life. In the dark, he cursed several times as he found himself again and again ankle deep in puddles of icy slush. A hundred yards up this increasingly dark passage, he found an even narrower and darker one, a blind alley branching off to the right again and almost blocked with piles of evil-smelling and rain-

147

soaked garbage. At the very entrance to this alley, he stopped by a dark doorway, rang a bell, and waited.

The door was soon opened by a very dark boy of eighteen or twenty whose hawklike profile and heavy-lidded eyes suggested that he might be a Kurd or an Iranian rather than a Turk. He was wearing a fancy pseudomilitary livery, that of a page boy or night club porter. But its gold braid was sorely tarnished, its blue-gray cloth and silk lapels were grimy from long wear, and the pants were sagging in the seat and the knees where they had long lost their tailored shape. Recognizing the Captain, the boy grinned cheerfully, then began to help him somewhat caressingly to remove his overcoat. Golden-haired and as handsome as an ancient Greek poet's description of a legendary hero, the Captain could not help attracting attention as a truly exotic figure as he now picked his way hesitantly through the crowd of much darker men and women assembled around low tables between the door and the bar that stood at the back of the tiny night club. Breathing its warmer air that was thick with tobacco smoke in which he could still distinguish an occasional more pungent whiff of hashish, he realized that he was already quite drunk. He had indeed been drinking steadily since early that evening, most of the time alone in his hotel room, out of boredom or to screw up courage for this outing.

Ali, the young porter, soon joined him, standing beside the Captain, who sat on a high stool, propped against the wall at the far end of the bar. Ali now placed his arm possessively around the Captain's waist, leaning against him sensuously with the whole weight of his slim but athletic body. The Captain could feel against his own thigh the proof of the boy's prompt physical desire, more truthful and explicit than gestures or words spoken in an unfamiliar language. The Captain ordered drinks and began to converse in English with the bald and barrel-chested bartender, a former merchant seaman who spoke fluent English in a deep throaty voice and had the build of a retired wrestler:

—Did you get me a hotel room?

—No, I didn't find time today. We had the cops here this

148

afternoon, questioning us about a customer who claims he had his wallet stolen from him here last night. But he was drunk when he came in, and he sat for an hour where you are now, with nobody near him who might have slipped a hand into his pocket. Anyhow, he first noticed he'd lost his wallet when he had to pay for his drinks, but I'm ready to bet he had already lost it somewhere else, before coming to bring us bad luck. *Mashallah,* we don't need that kind of customer who can't pay for his drinks and brings us the cops too the next day. I thought he had the Evil Eye the moment I first saw him over there in the doorway. But you can't turn them away on a hunch like that.

—But I gave you the money for the room last night and explained that I wanted one that is heated and has hot water too. I don't want to have to run around looking for hotel rooms at this hour, especially on a night like this and without being able to speak or understand a word of Turkish.

—I'll explain it all to Ali and give him your money. He'll know where to find you a room. It's easy, in any hotel around here.

The bartender began to explain it all in Turkish to Ali, after which he repeated to the Captain in English the result of this brief consultation:

—He'll take you to the Büyük Yenishehir Palas Oteli. It's a nice place, a new *turistik* hotel, heated and with hot water in every room, but with a Greek night porter who knows all about these things, *hamdullah*. Thank God, we still have a few wise guys like that in this city that will soon be fit only for angels. The night porter will ask you only to show your passport and to register. It'll cost you twenty-four *lirasi* for a double room, but you must tip him two or three *lirasi* so that Ali can join you upstairs without registering.

A few minutes later, the Captain left the bar with Ali, who shivered in his thin livery as he led the way through a maze of dark alleys to the lighted doorway of the hotel. There, they found that all the rooms were already occupied. The night porter, an unshaven old polyglot Greek who seemed to have

149

seen better days, explained to the Captain in lisping French that a football team from Izmir had descended that week end on Istanbul with all its local fans, for a match against the Besiktash team, so that all the less expensive but decent hotels in the neighborhood had been fully booked weeks ahead by an agency in Izmir. Perhaps Ali should be sent out in this foul weather to scout around for a room while the Captain waited here. The Captain agreed despondently, and Ali left him seated, in a plastic-upholstered armchair that smelled vaguely of acetone, in the Büyük Yenishehir Palas Oteli's narrow and brilliantly lit hallway. Nervously, the Captain threw away, in a tall nickel-plated standing ash tray, a half-smoked cigarette, but immediately lit another.

The night porter interrupted the Captain's meditations sympathetically in a mixed salad of lisping French, Greek, Turkish, and occasional English:

"Il est zentil, vot' p'tit ami." The Captain understood that the night porter wished to reassure him that Ali was a good boy. *"Prenez un kafezaki en attendant, Missié, et manzez un peu de mon ekmek kadaif.* Take it easy, as you say it in *Ingiliz.* Ali is an OK *Chodjuk, inshallah."* The Captain agreed that a cup of coffee might do him good. Within a few minutes, the night porter had produced a tiny cup of steaming and fragrant Turkish coffee and some sweet oriental pastry served on a garishly decorated glass plate. The Captain enjoyed this symbolical hospitality in silence.

Ali returned half an hour later. At first, he explained something at great length in Turkish to the night porter, who seemed to dismiss all of Ali's wordy arguments in a contemptuously peremptory tone, with the abrupt mannerisms of speech and gesture of a spiritual descendant of Homer and Plato who condescends to use Turkish syntax only if he can reduce it to the bare necessities of verbal communication. The night porter then summarized the whole situation for the Captain's benefit:

"Il n'a pas trouvé, mais il y a. He hasn't found a room, but there are rooms. *Il est zentil, mais c'est un villazois:* he's nice,

150

but a village boy. *Il ne connait pas Stamboul comme moi.* He doesn't know Istanbul as I do. *Allez, ze m'occupe de vous. Il y a, oui, il y a. Venez avec moi. Ali attend ici."*

The Captain understood that Ali was now to wait here at the hotel desk while the night porter ventured forth with him to find one of the many rooms that were still said to be available in this inhospitable night. Again, they wandered up and down narrow and slush-infested alleys, scattering ahead of them a few drenched rats or cats that had gathered around garbage cans, turning to the left or the right in what appeared to the Captain to be a veritable maze of deserted back streets extending between crowded and run-down apartment houses, from the Beyoglu terminal of the *Tunel* to the bluffs that overlook the Golden Horn. Finally, they stopped before the entrance to a tall and narrow-fronted apartment house.

The door was closed, and the Greek night porter rang a bell. When the Turkish doorman appeared a few minutes later in filthy cotton pajamas, the Captain's companion explained something to him in peremptory Turkish and instructed the Captain to tip him one lira. The Captain followed the Greek up a badly lit and narrow staircase to the door of a third-floor apartment where they stopped and rang a bell several times, as if tapping a message in Morse code.

There they waited a while before the door was opened by a fat young Levantine who was wearing brilliant red silk pajamas, drawn tight over his bulging body and revealing, between the strained buttons of the jacket, patches of an infelicitously hairy chest and belly which contrasted oddly with a pale and flabby face, still numb and expressionless as if sleep had made it swell with edema, but smeared with an incredible quantity of greenish and foul-smelling depilatory ointment. The Greek night porter began to explain the situation to the young Levantine in a mixture of Greek and lisping French. The young man laughed throatily, like an operatic prima donna practicing her trills, cast a coy glance at the Captain, and invited them both into the apartment with a sweeping gesture of his hand that revealed a

151

flashy gold bracelet stretched taut around a thick and hairy wrist: *"Ça fera dix lirettes, Monsieur. Merci."*

The Captain drew out his wallet and paid the required ten lira for the room, to which he was now led through a diminutive hallway and a small and crowded living room which proved to be a veritable apotheosis of Levantine bad taste in interior decoration and in Roman Catholic religious art. The flowered and faded paper of its walls was plastered with cheap and garish reproductions of Italian old-master representations of the Virgin and of various Saints. Ormolu crucifixes and majolica fonts for Holy Water were interspersed among them, but all of this was paradoxically facing, on another wall, an elaborately framed set of cheaply elegant and mildly erotic prints published some thirty years earlier in Paris or in Vienna. The room's heavy but torn and soiled damask window drapes and its numerous battered pieces of overelaborate rococo furniture all looked moreover as if they had been looted from half a dozen different homes after an earthquake, or gradually salvaged, bit by bit, from pawnshops and auctions.

Reached through a glass door from this cluttered living room, the bedroom itself was furnished in similar taste, but with a profusion of potted plants balanced precariously on unsteady and contorted turn-of-the-century whatnots, and, on the mantel piece and a couple of dressers, of groups of stuffed birds and butterflies mounted among artificial flowers under huge glass globes.

The Captain's Greek guide left him here, promising to return with Ali in a few minutes. Alone in the bedroom, the Captain removed his overcoat and threw it over the back of an overstuffed rococo armchair. The double bed, a huge French-style "battlefield," was tumultuously unmade, its soiled sheets and torn silk eiderdown-stuffed coverlet none too inviting. He felt less and less inclined to pursue his orginal purpose, but was interrupted in his hesitations by a knock on the door. His host had returned, bringing him another steaming *kafezaki* and fresh linen to make the bed worthy of a paying guest. To put him at his ease, the fat

152

young Levantine made a few coy remarks in French about the Captain's rare good looks. Somehow, he sounded like an impecunious widowed mother flattering desperately a desirable prospect for her marriageable daughter.

Once the bed was made, they waited together for Ali to ring the doorbell. The fat young Levantine, a vaguely Italian dressmaker, was a gossipy "queen" of the kind that one meets in any big city, though they tend perhaps to be more degraded in Istanbul than elsewhere, more vulgarly feminine and less presumptuously "elegant," probably because Turkish prejudices and contempt allow them less scope for any illusions of grandeur. Another half hour went by as the young Levantine prattled less and less merrily, since the Captain answered him, if at all, but vaguely or laconically. At last, the Greek hotel porter returned alone, somewhat flushed from hastening up the three flight of stairs:

"Il est parti, vot' zentil ami. La police est venue contrôler le rezistr' à l'hotel. Ali n'avait pas ses papiers. On l'a emmené au Karaköl. Ça fera dix lirettes pour moi, pour le dérangement. Merci, bonne nuit, et amusez-vous bien."

The Captain began to wonder whether all of this was true. Had the police really made, while he and the night-porter were on their way, a routine check of the Büyük Yenishehir Palas Oteli's guest register? Had they really found Ali without any identification papers and taken him off to the police station for further investigation? Or had all this been but a devious plot to separate him from Ali and force him to spend the night and his money with this fat Levantine queen? As soon as he received, for his troubles, the ten lira that he had requested, the night porter vanished hastily, wishing the Captain a good night and lots of fun. The Captain was now alone in the bedroom with the young Levantine, who sat nervously giggling on the edge of the bed, as if waiting for a cue. To his host's surprise, the Captain grabbed his hat and overcoat, rammed the hat down on his head, rushed out of the bedroom as he was still buttoning the overcoat, and was gone without saying a word of explanation or

153

farewell, not even demanding a refund of the money he had paid for the use of the room. Downstairs, in the street, the Captain soon found his way back to Beyoglu, hailed a passing cab, and drove despondently to his hotel, beyond Taksim Park. There, for the next few days of his leave, he remained closeted in a room like that of any first-class American hotel, drinking heavily in his self-imposed solitude.

THREE FAITHS, ONE GOD

In one of the boxes of secondhand books that the Latin Quarter dealers of Paris display on the parapets of the embankments of the Seine, I once picked up an old guidebook of Istanbul. It attracted my attention because it contained more explanatory text and fewer illustrations than those that are now published for hasty semiliterate and camera-clicking tourists who know things only by sight, and, no longer finding enough time for reading, generally remain a mine of misinformation about all that they have seen. To prepare myself for a more thorough exploration of the Byzantine and Ottoman monuments of the former Turkish capital, I therefore began to read this book a couple of months before I was actually able to leave Paris for Turkey. Somewhere among the learned author's very factual descriptions of Byzantine churches and other Greek-Orthodox monuments, I found a story that fascinated me because it contrasted so oddly with the otherwise sober tone of his historical explanations.

In 1453, when the besieged Byzantine capital finally fell to the Turks, it had been resisting their attacks for so long that

155

most of the surrounding territory was already living fairly peace-fully behind the Turkish lines. Close to the besieged city, a Greek-Orthodox monastery thus went about its daily business without ever being disturbed by constant warfare which seemed to have become part of the natural order of things. Among its bearded and black-robed brethren, it harbored a particularly lazy, gluttonous, and ignorant monk who never displayed much interest in anything but the immediate satisfaction of his own gross appetite. Brother Dositheos, since we must give him a name, happened one day to be preparing to fry himself some fish in a pan when a breathless messenger reached the monas-tery, bringing news that the Imperial city had at long last fallen to the Turks.

"Impossible," Brother Dositheos replied, calmly continuing to season his fish, perhaps even sprinkling a pinch of oregano herbs in the pan while the rest of the monastery interrupted their occupations to listen in dismay to the messenger's account of bloodshed, plunder, and rape. "Impossible," Brother Dositheos repeated. "Haven't we all seen them displaying every day for weeks, on their rounds along the top of the city's battlements, all the miraculous ikons under whose protection the city has been placed by our saintly Patriarch Gennadios? Haven't we all heard that the Patriarch has revolted against the usurping authority of the new Roman Legate and proclaimed again the full independence of our Church? How can you believe that the Most Holy Virgin and all our Saints have deserted a city thus placed under their protection?"

The messenger and the other monks continued to argue with Brother Dositheos while he began to fry his fish as if nothing of any importance had happened. Finally, he rebuked them: "I'll believe you if the fish that I'm now frying come back to life in my pan."

Immediately, the three fish that he was frying jumped out of the pan, live and unharmed, and fell into the waters of a nearby pool that was fed by a natural spring. But all three fish bore, on one side, black marks where their skin had already been charred by the pan, whereas their other side remained silvery and unharmed. Ever since, there has always been, in the monastery's pool, which has thus become a *haghiasma* of waters that perform miraculous cures, the same number of fish that continue to display the same unique markings.

I decided to investigate this tale in Istanbul and, shortly after my arrival there, repeated it to a friend, a well-known Turkish historian. He too was fascinated by it, but admitted that he had never yet heard of the monastery and its miraculous pool. Inquiries made in various quarters then revealed that a few older people could remember having once heard the legend of the miraculous fish, but nobody that I knew had ever seen them or could tell me where the monastery and its pool might still be found.

In my wanderings in the more distant section of Old Istanbul where the last Byzantine Emperors had lived in the Vlachernae Palace, I asked again and again, in the following weeks, whether anyone there knew where I might find the *balikli kilisi,* the Church of the Fish. Many had heard of it and informed me that it was somewhere beyond the city's battlements, but nobody could tell me near which gate I might find it along the great fortified stretch that protected the city from land attacks all the way from the shores of the Golden Horn to those of the Sea of Marmara, where the city was then defended against attacks from the sea by the sinister Fortress of the Seven Towers.

Though I still failed to find the object of my search, the search itself proved fruitful, however, in that it now led me to discover a number of little-known mosques and Byzantine monuments which I might otherwise have neglected. I was thus encouraged to continue my explorations, especially as the spring weather was ideal for such long walks in little-frequented neighborhoods on the outskirts of Old Istanbul, where the fruit trees were blossoming in the many gardens scattered among almost rural slums and the ruins of abandoned monuments.

Among other monuments, I then discovered, close to the Fortress of the Seven Towers where I had just visited the dun-

157

geons and deciphered on their walls some of the messages left there by desperate prisoners, the ruins of what is now called Imrahor Djami, the Mosque of the Executioner. Situated among unidentifiable Byzantine ruins which an old Turkish woman with a passion for flowers, cats, and caged songbirds had transformed into a fantastic garden that she watered diligently with rain from a well-head that still communicated with vast underground Byzantine cisterns, this abandoned Byzantine church had once been rebuilt as a mosque by the pious executioner employed at the nearby fortress. It had previously been attached to the Monastery of Saint John of Studion, reputed in ecclesiastical history to have been the first Christian monastic community endowed with a rule, as opposed to earlier communities of hermits grouped together without having a common rule of life.

One day, close to one of the gates of the Old City, I then discovered another old mosque that was not listed in any of my guidebooks. It had been built to commemorate a holy man who, on the day that Baghdad had fallen to the armies of the Sultan, had stood there proclaiming the great news by the gate of the city, having been vouchsafed a vision of the fall of Baghdad, though the messengers sent to the Ottoman capital to bring the news of victory reached Istanbul only several weeks later, having come all the way from Baghdad by camel or on horseback.

In any other city, this little mosque might have attracted the tourist's attention. Though its proportions were modest, its architecture was in the same delicately classical style as the famous Baghdad Kiosk in the gardens of the Imperial Palace of Top Kapu. Its decoration was more simple, but in exquisite taste, and its *mihrab,* toward which the Faithful turn when they must face the east in prayer, was of finely carved marble and flanked with beautiful flowered panels of brightly colored Iznik ceramic tiles. As I was quietly admiring all this, I was approached by the mosque's *Imam,* a surprisingly young Moslem ecclesiastic for these days of weakened faith when so few men of his generation choose a religious way of life. As he greeted me, he seemed to be proud to discover a foreigner visiting his otherwise deserted mosque. In broken Turkish, I told him that I found the *mihrab* truly beautiful, *chok güzel*. Seeing that I was bareheaded but wore an embroidered cap that I always carry in my pocket for such occasions, and that I had dutifully removed my shoes before entering the sacred precincts, he asked me if I was a Moslem. When I told him without further ado that I'm a Jew, an American poet, he remarked that we are all brothers if we still believe in one and the same God, especially in days when all too many men have lost their faith.

Suddenly, it occurred to me that he might know where I could find the *balikli kilisi*. To my inquiry, he replied that he knew it well. One of the Greek priests there was his friend. I would find the monastery only about half a mile from here, just beyond the nearest gate in the Old City's battlements. He then decided to lock the door of his mosque and accompany me to the gate, where he pointed out to me, in the suburban country-side beyond it, a few buildings that were almost concealed be-hind a slight tree-capped rising that was skirted by a rough road leading from the walled city's gate.

Together, we followed this road till we reached a group of monumental buildings that appeared to have been built in the early nineteenth century, in the Russian neo-Classical style of many Greek Orthodox monasteries that I had already visited on Mount Athos or elsewhere in Greece. Wealthy and pious Rus-sians once devoted vast sums to the task of rebuilding such hal-lowed ecclesiastical monuments which, since the fall of Byzan-tium, had slowly been allowed to go to rack and ruin. But these particular buildings now seemed to have fallen on evil days again. At first, they appeared to be deserted, left almost in a state of ruin. Suddenly, a black-robed Greek ecclesiastic ap-peared in a doorway. Recognizing my guide, he greeted him cordially and volubly in fluent Turkish. I was then introduced to him somewhat abruptly as an American Jew, a poet who be-lieved in God and who had come to visit the *haghiasma*.

The Greek priest led us through a paved yard where grass grew between the disjointed stone flags, to a huge church built

159

in neo-Classical Russian imitation of a pillared Greek temple. Unlocking its main door, he revealed to me its once majestic and splendidly decorated aisles, which now offered every evidence of having but recently been wrecked by a mob of sacrilegious Vandals. From the vaulted ceilings, heavily wrought brass lamps had been torn and still lay scattered on the floor. The painted *iconostasis,* or icon screen, with its neo-Gothic woodwork and its saints depicted in the "Pre-Raphaelite" manner of Russian Romantic painters who studied in Rome instead of remaining faithful to traditional Byzantine styles, was sorely battered. Though much had already been hastily repaired, I could see that great effort and expense would still be necessary in order to restore all that had been so wantonly destroyed or damaged.

We stood there for a while, embarrassed by what we saw and by the Greek priest's silent sorrow as he contemplated the ruin of the splendid church of which he had once been so proud. Then he sighed, shrugged his shoulders and, through another door, led us into a small walled churchyard where all the marble tombs had been desecrated, disfigured, or overturned. From their Greek inscriptions, I was able to read the names of a couple of nineteenth-century Patriarchs of Constantinople as well as of several formerly aristocratic Phanariot families: Photiadis, Zarifi, Eliasco, Mavrogordato. In a corner of the yard, a pile of human bones had been gathered, after the Turkish mob had torn them from their sepulchers and scattered them to the winds during the anti-Greek riots which the Menderes government encouraged, a few years earlier, as an expression of protest against Greek oppression of the Turkish minority in Cyprus.

The Greek priest patted the young *Imam's* shoulder affectionately, then explained to me in Turkish: "When he heard that the mob was coming here, he came and fetched us and hid us all in his mosque. God will remember what he did for us on that dreadful day."

Returning to one of the other buildings of the almost deserted monastery, the Greek priest opened a small and nondescript

160

door, then led us down some steps to a marble-lined and quite undamaged crypt that had escaped the attentions of the mob. In the marble basin of a fountain into which the waters of the natural spring now flowed, the three fish were swimming. They had black markings on one side, as if they had been burned, but their other side was immaculately silvery. The miraculous fish seemed to have lived over four hundred years, ever since the fall of Byzantium, and only recently to have escaped by another miracle the destructive frenzy of a rioting Turkish mob. I felt down my spine a shiver, like the devastating touch of the finger of God in a poem by Gerard Manley Hopkins. We stood there, all three, in silence, each one of us confirmed in his own different faith, but united in our common respect for all who try sincerely to be worthy of their faith.

THE VAMPIRES OF ISTANBUL:
A STUDY IN MODERN COMMUNICATIONS METHODS

Yeni Aksham, Istanbul, 7 February 1960, front page:

Our readers will be justifiably shocked to hear that cases of vampirism can still occur in the heart of a modern metropolis like Istanbul. Yesterday morning, the police of our city was suddenly called upon to investigate such a case and promptly arrested the chief culprit, Mahmut Osmanoglu, a carter, 48 years old, a native of Edirne, living in Fener at Küchük Gülhane Djaddesi 37.

While giving her ten-year-old son Hasan his weekly bath, Füreya Öztürk, a mother of five children living at Küchük Gülhane Djaddesi 11, noticed yesterday a suspicious scar on the child's upper arm. She recognized it at once as the mark left by the needle of a hypodermic syringe and began to question the boy. He then admitted that he and two of his companions had been accosted in the street the day before by an older man who promised to give them sweetmeats if they accompanied him to

162

his room. The three boys agreed, in their innocence, and found themselves offered by the carter to two other vampires who had been waiting for him there while he went out to recruit their victims.

Hasan described to his mother in great detail the orgy of vampirism which then took place. The three men produced hypodermic syringes with which each one extracted blood from the upper arm of his chosen victim, after which they drank this blood from ordinary tea glasses with great relish while the boys were given cordials and sweetmeats to help them recover from their fright.

Accompanied by her son, Füreya Öztürk went immediately to the nearest police station in the Fener district of our city, where she is well known as a respectable housewife, the pensioned widow of a Turkish war hero who was killed in Korea while fighting the Communists. To the sympathetic local police captain, she repeated her atrocious story. Quite understandably, the poor woman was in tears, as the police captain subsequently told our reporter. Two policemen, Muzafer Tavukdjuoglu and Ali Hamit, were sent out at once to investigate the case. Fortunately, the boy could still remember the house where he had been a victim of this disgusting orgy of vampirism. He was able to lead the police upstairs to the door of the very room which had been the scene of the crime. But the door was locked and the police found nobody there. Inquiries in the neighborhood revealed that the carter Mahmut Osmanoglu was probably still at work but could generally be found at home later in the evening.

The police waited till seven o'clock and then came again and found the carter alone in the lodging where he generally lives with his mother. He had just returned from work and, faced with an account of his crime, denied it. He admitted, however, that he and his two companions had practiced unnatural vices with the three boys and recompensed them as usual with sweetmeats. The three boys, he claimed, were regular visitors to his room, where they seemed to take pleasure in his company and

163

in that of his friends. Mahmut Osmanoglu was then arrested on the charge of vampirism and the case is being investigated.

Yeni Aksham, 8 February 1960, p. 3, local news.

Mahmut Osmanoglu, the Vampire of Fener, has been unable or unwilling to identify for the police the two other vampires who perpetrated with him the disgusting crimes which we reported yesterday. After several hours of interrogation at the local police station and later at police headquarters, he finally alleged that he knew only one of the other two vampires, a member of our city's police force who visits him frequently in his lodging in the evening, often bringing an anonymous companion and threatening to arrest the carter for some past crime if he refuses to go out and recruit young victims for their orgies of blood-drinking. Police headquarters deny the validity of the carter's story, pointing out that it is an obvious attempt to discourage any further move on their part to uncover what now appears to be a secret network of vampires operating in this city.

Yeni Aksham, 10 February 1960, p. 3.

A second case of vampirism has been reported from Langna, where two young mothers saw an unknown old woman approach their little daughters in the street and offer sweetmeats to the children. The old woman was attacked and beaten by the indignant mothers and was already lying unconscious in the street when the police reached the scene of the incident and intervened. As it was impossible to question her on account of her condition, the woman was taken to hospital, pending further investigation of the matter. She has meanwhile been identified as Meriam Terzibashjian, 72 years of age, a native of Elazig and a widow, presently employed as a cleaning woman in the kitchens of the Armenian hospital in Psamatia.

164

Yeni Aksham, 12 February 1960, p. 1 of the Weekly Literary and Scientific Supplement.

We have pleasure in offering to our readers today a scientific study on vampirism by Professor Reshat Allalemdji, the well-known authority whose recent proposals, for solving Istanbul's traffic problems by reducing the frequency of accident-proneness by psychoanalyzing all convicted violators of traffic regulations, caused so much comment when we published them here a few weeks ago. Professor Allalemdji studied medicine at Leipzig University, where a special course on vampirism is an integral part of the training of all medical students in the neuropsychiatric clinic of this world-famous university.—The Editors

Though fortunately rare as a vice or as what we scientists who are not moralists prefer to call a mental disease, vampirism is one of those evils that have continued to plague mankind since the very dawn of civilization. There exist among us a number of unfortunate men and women whose physical health requires that they absorb regularly certain quantities of fresh human blood. If deprived of this diet, they die within a few days of a rare kind of pernicious anemia for which no adequate cure has yet been discovered. Whether their dread disease is hereditary or not, we may never be able to ascertain, cases of vampirism being fortunately so rare that it has so far proven impossible to compare and investigate them scientifically. Besides, most vampires, when caught and questioned, remain extremely reticent about their ghoulish habits.

For many centuries, our knowledge of vampirism was thus founded almost exclusively on a few legendary cases that have so shocked popular imagination that they have been committed to memory in ballads, fairy tales, and other forms of folklore. The well-known story of Little Red Ridinghood and the Wolf is thus but a disguised account of a legendary French case of vampirism. The famous German poet Goethe also refers to a case of vampirism, probably of German origin, in his poem entitled *Der Erlkönig.*

165

Modern anthropology has revealed, however, that "where there is smoke there must also be fire," and that folklore and legends are the repository of truths which have survived orally from prehistoric times when man was not yet able to record in writing the facts that he had observed. Subsequent generations gradually distorted or embellished these facts with the inevitable inaccuracies of oral tradition. Legendary tales of vampirism are therefore being investigated scientifically by modern anthropologists in order to find out whether we have to deal here with a mental or physical disease, or perhaps with the clandestine practices of some secret cannibalistic religious cult. The present case of the vampires of Fener may thus offer Turkish scientists a rare opportunity to study in real life and at first hand what they all too often know only from the very secondary sources of published folklore and legend.

Fortunately, history has already recorded two famous cases of vampirism which led to sensational trials in periods which have left us reliable firsthand documents. The first of these cases is that of Gilles de Rais (1404–40), a man who was a Marshal of France and the companion of arms of Joan of Arc. After her trial and execution on a false accusation of witchcraft, he appears to have become, in spite of his distinguished military past and the responsibilities of his position, involved in the most disgusting practices of sorcery. At the time of his arrest and trial in Nantes, it was proven beyond dispute that he had already tortured and murdered at least eight hundred male adolescents. Though it was alleged by the prosecution that he sacrificed them to the Devil in the course of criminal Black Masses, it is now generally agreed that he was a vampire and that the elaborate ceremonies which he conducted served only as a setting for obscene sacraments in the course of which he drank the blood of his young victims.

The second case, that of Countess Elizabeth Batthyani (1580–1640), occurred in Hungary. At the time of her trial, it was proven that she had enticed over six hundred attractive peasant girls into her castle, from which not one of them had ever been

166

seen to return alive. Witnesses at her trial testified that, whenever she saw a beautiful young girl, her mouth literally watered so that the saliva could be seen dripping from her chin. Ever since the horrible revelations of her trial, human vampires have been believed to exist in quite large numbers in certain rural areas of Hungary, where cases of vampirism have again and again been denounced to the authorities, especially in those disputed frontier provinces, such as Transylvania and the Banat, where the feudal landowners were Hungarian nobles who ruthlessly exploited their Slavic or Rumanian serfs.

The Turkish vampires whose shocking practices have recently been revealed may thus prove, on further investigation, to be descendants of Hungarian vampires who came and settled in Istanbul when Hungary was still a province of our glorious Ottoman Empire, which might then add grist to the mills of those scientists who believe vampirism to be a hereditary disease. In any case, vampirism appears to be something utterly alien to our national character, since we find no mention of it in our native Turkish or Turanian folklore.

Professor Fakir Allalemdji
Psychiatrist,
Bakirköy Mental Hospital

Yeni Aksham, 14 February 1960, p. 3.

The police continues to investigate the case of the vampires of Fener, diligently seeking to identify the two unknown accomplices who participated with the carter Mahmut Osmanoglu in the scenes of vampirism which he organized for them in his room. Yesterday, the three boys who had been victims of the orgy of drinking human blood that we had reported were brought face to face with the carter. Two of the boys failed to recognize him, declaring that they had never seen him before, which seems scarcely likely as they happen to be his neighbors, living in the same street where everyone knows everyone else, at least by sight. But these two boys also refuse to admit ever having been victims of any orgy of vampirism.

Only Hasan Öztürk continues to assert that he and his two companions had accompanied the carter to his lodging and met two other men there, after which the three older men took blood from the boys with hypodermic syringes and drank it fresh in tea glasses. Pressed by the police for a more detailed description of these two other men, Hasan Öztürk, who had already recognized and identified the carter Mahmut Osmanoglu as the man who first accosted him and the two other boys in the street and who organized in his room the whole orgy, now gave the following description of the two unidentified culprits. One of them is tall and dark, about twenty-five years of age, wears a mustache and looks like the goalkeeper of the Fenerbahtche football team. The other is some ten years older and looks like the German film star Curd Jurgens. Police inquiries reveal, however, that Hamdi Kotcha, the well-known goalkeeper of the Fenerbahtche football team, was absent from Istanbul on the day of the crime, having accompanied his team to Izmir where they won a match against a team from Marash. Nor is the German film star Curd Jurgens recorded by our passport controls to have entered the country within the last two years, so that it is presumed that this may be a case of mistaken identities.

Yeni Aksham, Istanbul, 19 February 1960, Letter to the Editor, p. 3 of the Weekly Literary and Scientific Supplement.

Dear Sir,

I have been a faithful reader of *Yeni Aksham* for the past twenty years and have nearly always found myself warmly applauding its courageous and enlightened stand on all national issues. I was therefore all the more shocked when I read, in your issue of 12 February last, Dr. Allalemdji's deliberately obscurantist article on vampirism. Surely, such a sop thrown to the

168

senile believers in the positivist historical science of fifty or more years ago was unworthy of a progressive newspaper.

I will take issue only on three points raised by Dr. Allalemdji in his article:

Firstly, all serious and objective students of medieval history now know, from the documents which have survived, what vested interests in religious prejudice and in reactionary feudalism were at work to conceal the real issues at stake in the trial of Gilles de Rais so as to avoid discrediting an outstanding member of the nobility in the eyes of its enemies. Gilles de Rais never practiced vampirism but was accused of it in order to cover up his other crimes. A homosexual debauchee, he had abducted countless young serfs from their modest peasant homes to serve him in his disgraceful orgies. But he soon tired of each one of them in turn and, instead of then allowing them to return to their villages and spread there the report of his debaucheries, he preferred to castrate them and sell them as eunuchs to the Arab princes of the Maghreb. The Catholic Church, of course, could not tolerate the idea that Christians were thus being sold, beneath its very nose, by a Christian noble to more enlightened and less cruel Moslem masters, so that the truth was hushed up and a less politically dangerous accusation of vampirism formulated.

Secondly, reliable scholars have recently discovered in Hungary some of the documents of the trial of the infamous Countess Elizabeth Batthyani. From these it appears clearly that she was a paid agent of the Ottoman court, recruiting Hungarian peasant girls, famous for their milk, as wet nurses for unwanted Christian children saved from dying of exposure when their parents abandoned them. These children were being charitably brought up in Moslem orphanages to serve later as Janissaries in our Imperial regiments of converts to Islam. Here again, the Catholic Church and its feudal supporters refused to admit that such a clandestine trade existed in provinces that it claimed to control; again, it preferred to trump up a charge of vampirism, though the Countess was known to suck milk from her victims and never blood, since she insisted on testing each one of them

169

herself and had even acquired a somewhat infantile taste for human milk, which also explains why her mouth is reported to have watered at the mere sight of an opulent bosom.

On both these points, I am prepared to quote, should Dr. Allalemdji desire, all the relevant bibliographical sources in recent French or Hungarian scholarly publications. My third point is one of principle rather than of historical scholarship. Dr. Allalemdji quotes us cases of vampirism in which six hundred and even eight hundred victims were alleged to have been killed. In the recent Fener case, not a single victim has yet been reported to be missing or can be presumed to have been killed. Can the Fener case be compared in any way with these classical if somewhat unreliable cases of vampirism?

Sincerely yours,
Turgut Ekmekdjioglu
Professor of European History
Istanbul University

Yeni Aksham, 19 February 1960, Letter to the Editor, same page as the preceding one.

Dear Sir,

For many years I have deplored, like other devout patriots, the Godless policies of the successive governments of our unfortunate Republic. The present Fener case of vampirism proves how right I have been.

Had our nation remained faithful to its Moslem traditions, Turks of today would not have acquired as they have a taste for the red meat of animals which have not been slaughtered according to the strict rules of our religion. One sin leads to another and guzzling underdone steaks like the Infidels at the Istanbul Hilton Hotel or elsewhere in our increasingly degenerate cities has now led some of our more decadent compatriots to acquire a taste for human blood too. No restaurant in Turkey should be allowed to serve European-style steaks, especially that

170

typically Infidel dish that is so blasphemously called Steak Tartare, as if our Moslem Tartar brethren could be suspected of ever having made a practice of eating anything as monstrously unclean.

Sincerely yours,
Hodja Ibrahim Hadjikaraosmanoglu

Yeni Aksham, Istanbul, 26 February 1960, Letter to the Editor, same page as the preceding letter.

Dear Sir,

I have read with great interest Dr. Allalemdji's article and the curious correspondence that it has provoked in your columns. All this reveals how ignorant most Turks have become of Turcology in general and, in particular, of the ancient customs and beliefs of our Turanian ancestors.

Let me assure you and your readers, as a professor of Turanian and Turkish folklore, that vampirism is an ancient and honorable Turkish and Turanian custom, originally a form of medicine once practiced in Central Asia by Shamanistic priests before our ancestors were converted to Islam. By sucking the sick blood out of their patients, these Shamanistic priests cured them of their diseases, all illnesses being, according to their doctrine, diseases of the blood.

Sincerely yours,
Turhan Tashkent
Professor of Turcology
University of Ankara

Yeni Aksham, 4 March 1960, Letter to the Editor, p. 3 of the Weekly Literary and Scientific Supplement.

Dear Sir,

Professor Tashkent is perfectly right. I come of a family that has for countless generations earned an honest livelihood, even

171

after its conversion to Islam, by practicing Shamanistic medicinal vampirism in the Vilayet of Afyon Karahissar. When I was still a boy, long before my parents moved to Istanbul where my father subsequently became a well-known pedicure, I used to see hundreds of sick people brought to our house by their family and friends for treatment at the hands of my grandfather. He was generally content to accept modest fees and had specialized in the treatment of obesity. Our home had thus become a kind of clinic where my grandfather's cures of vampirism saved many a high Ottoman dignitary from becoming an ungainly old man and the laughingstock of his inferiors. When Turks of the more privileged classes began to go abroad for more expensive and often less effective cures in well-publicized European watering places, my father solved the problem of our dwindling family practice by moving to Istanbul and setting himself up as a pedicure in the Passage in Beyoglu, where he still cured many a badly infected toe, however, by merely sucking it. I am sure that a number of your older readers will still remember having been treated by him.

Sincerely yours,
Boghatsch Hakimoglu

Yeni Aksham, Istanbul, 4 March 1960, same page as preceding letter.

Dear Sir,

As President of the Pan-Turanian Association of Shamanistic Vampires, I have been authorized by a quorum of our National Board to applaud and corroborate on its behalf every word of Professor Tashkent's remarkably objective letter. All our members have graduated from the last existing schools of ancient Shamanistic medicine. In Turkey, the last of these schools is now situated in Urfa, in Anatolia; in recent years, we have no longer received any correspondence from the schools which still existed in the Russian Turkestan before the Soviet Revolution, so that

172

we are not able to report on the present state of our science in Soviet Russia, where it may have been suppressed as a manifestation of Pan-Turanian nationalism in the course of the Stalinist persecutions which decimated the Moslem intelligentsia of the Central Asian Soviet Republics.

Our school in Urfa had first been founded and endowed in the thirteenth century by Korkhut Seljuk, one of the last of the ruling princes of the Oghuz Beylik. Though our faculty still graduates a few selected Shamanistic physicians every year, these are now trained only in the theory of their science, without any practical experience of the treatment of human patients, if only to avoid all possible conflicts with existing Turkish laws regulating the practice of medicine. As an association, we therefore limit our activities to the organization of campaigns to promote a more enlightened appreciation of the value of our science and thus hope soon to obtain public support for changes in our legislation in order to prevent our venerable and valuable science from becoming extinct.

Yours sincerely,
Tchinghiz Hulaghuoglu

Yeni Aksham, Istanbul, 4 March 1960, same page as preceding letter.

Dear Sir,

I hope other readers of *Yeni Aksham* have realized, as I did at once, that all these countless cases of shameless vampirism which now disgrace our once beautiful and peaceful city in the eyes of the civilized world are the work of a small but well organized band of fanatical Armenians. It has long been known that Armenians require the blood of Moslem children to prepare the meat pies that they eat at their annual Easter celebrations. All too often, they have relied in the past on corrupt Turkish or Kurdish accomplices to procure them their victims. My point is proven by the fact that an Armenian hag who works in the kitchens of the Armenian hospital has also been arrested in the present campaign to eradicate this wave of terrorism which, as always, is seasonal. Though Turks, the other vampires were surely employed as her agents.

Sincerely yours,
Atilla Bayraktutan

Yeni Aksham, Istanbul, 4 March 1960, same page as preceding letter.

Dear Sir,

I'm a hospital nurse and midwife. In all these stories about vampires, one thing worries me. How could the mother of one of the three victims recognize immediately the mark on her son's arm as having been left there by a hypodermic syringe? Unless she had special training as a nurse, how could she distinguish it from a mere scratch or a flea bite?

Respectfully yours,
Fazilet Bashkurt

Yeni Aksham, Istanbul, 4 March 1960, same page as preceding letter.

Dear Sir,

My kind Turkish neighbor is writing this letter for me because I never attended a Turkish school and have learned to write only Italian in the old days. Because I am a Christian, some Turkish vampires think they can steal my cats with impunity but we all worship one and the same God and there is justice now in our glorious Republic for all its citizens, regardless of race or religion. My cats are very beautiful and well fed and in the past ten years three of them have disappeared. I know that they have been victims of vampires and now my good Turkish neighbor shares my suspicion but we don't know what we should do about it. Isn't it illegal to steal cats and drink their blood like the blood

174

of human beings? Are they the same vampires who drink the blood of both or are there two kinds of vampires, those who drink human blood and those who drink the blood of cats? Perhaps Professor Allalemdji can answer my questions.

Sincerely yours,
Daria Genovesi

Yeni Aksham, Istanbul, 6 March 1960, p. 3, local news.

The case of the vampires of Fener is still being diligently investigated by the police. Prompted by the interest which so many of our readers have displayed, our reporter went yesterday to police headquarters to find out what progress has been made in solving this remarkable mystery. As we had previously reported, Hamdi Kotcha, the well-known goalkeeper of the Fenerbahtche football team, was able to supply a satisfactory alibi when Hasan Öztürk, one of the victims of the vampires, described him as one of the three men who had participated in this orgy of drinking human blood. Hamdi Kotcha happened on that day to be with his team in Izmir, playing a match against a team from Marash. Through Interpol, our police has now been able to ascertain that the German film star Curd Jurgens happened that day to be working in a Hollywood studio, so that he too has now submitted a satisfactory alibi.

The boy Hasan Öztürk remains the only witness of the actual orgies of vampirism which his mother, on the basis of his reports, denounced to the police. The other two boys whom he named as witnesses and co-victims continue to deny that the alleged vampires drank their blood. For lack of sufficiently conclusive evidence, the public prosecutor may therefore be obliged to drop the case against the carter Mahmut Osmanoglu, the only vampire who has so far been identified and who is now under arrest. Though Mahmut Osmanoglu has meanwhile admitted having practiced unnatural vices with the three boys, the latter and their parents hotly deny any such degenerate tendencies in their families. For lack of a complaint, the public prosecutor cannot prosecute Mahmut Osmanoglu for the only crime that he has so far confessed.

As for the other vampire, the Armenian cleaning woman Meriam Terzibashjian suspected of ·attempted vampirism in Langna, we regret to report that she died yesterday in the Armenian Hospital without having sufficiently recovered from her injuries, since February 10th, to be questioned by the police. Though all these investigations have so far proven to be somewhat confusing, it is believed at police headquarters that we may soon expect sensational revelations concerning the wave of vampirism that has swept our city.

Yeni Aksham, Istanbul, 11 March 1960, Letter to the Editor, p. 3 of the Weekly Literary and Scientific Supplement.

Dear Sir,

I am an unmarried mother and support myself, my little girl, and my invalid mother on my earnings as a *tchivtiteli* dancer. I used to earn high fees in the most expensive night clubs in Beyoglu and many of your readers will remember the film in which I starred, *The Girl with the Golden Belly*. It told the story of my life and was elected as the most popular Turkish film of the year for the Berlin Film Festival. Unfortunately, a jury of foreigners in Berlin was unable to understand the significance of *The Girl with the Golden Belly* as an artistic milestone in the history of the emancipation of Turkish womanhood, so it failed to get a prize.

But this was not my only misfortune in that year when my stars gave me every indication that I should stay at home and never expose myself unnecessarily to alien forces and influences. One winter night, as I was walking home from work, I slipped on the ice of the frozen Beyoglu sidewalk and fell and injured my hip. My left buttock soon began to swell and is now much larger than my right buttock. I have tried every medical treatment available, but modern science has been of no assistance. My professional life is now ruined. When I dance the *tchivtiteli,* men only laugh at me and I'm lucky if I find work in a low waterfront café in Tophane instead of the better Beyoglu nightclubs. Can you recommend me a reliable Shamanistic vampire whose treatments might solve my problem?

Sincerely yours,
Djevrieh Holivutlu

Yeni Aksham, Istanbul, 11 March 1960, p. 3 of the Weekly Literary and Scientific Supplement.

Dear Sir,

I'm a devout Moslem and was shocked to read your Christian correspondent's suggestion that Turks could kill and eat cats. After all the years she has lived in Turkey, Daria Genovesi, who appears to be a Turkish citizen, should really know that our Prophet taught us to respect cats above all other animals. No devout Turk, for instance, will ever drown a kitten, as the Infidels so frequently do. If there exist Turkish vampires that live on the blood of cats, they must surely be Kurdish Yazids who worship fire and the Devil. But with the constant influx of ignorant Anatolian villagers who seek work in our city, I would not be surprised to hear that Istanbul now harbors a secret community of Kurdish Yazids.

Another explanation for the disappearance of your correspondent's three cats might be that they were not really cats but cannibalistic were-mice, in fact mice that adopt the appearance of cats only during the daytime and resume their natural form as mice at night. It is a scientific fact that colonies of mice which have become too numerous for their own convenience then regulate their population by means of cannibalistic massacres. Some of the survivors, however, become were-mice and continue to prey on other mice. But it sometimes happens that were-mice also get attacked and killed by real cats. I witnessed such a case once with my own eyes. I was living in Cairo in a house that was infested by mice, in an old building in Mousky. I acquired a cat, but she could not cope with the situation. All she ever did was eat, sleep and purr. One day, I bought some poison and placed pieces of poisoned cheese at strategic points on the floor in the kitchen. When I came home late that night from the movies, I found a dead mouse on the floor near the kitchen sink. Instead of picking it up and throwing it at once into the garbage can, I left it there and went to bed. The next morning, in the middle of the kitchen floor where I had seen the dead mouse, I found the corpse of my cat. It was perhaps a were-mouse which, while it had been a mouse again at night, had eaten the poison and died; but at dawn its body had then assumed the form of a cat. Or had it died from eating a poisoned mouse? Were-mice are very rare, however, and your correspondent's story of her vanished cats would constitute the first recorded case of a cat-lover being afflicted with three were-mice. May I ask your correspondent if her three lost cats happened to be of the same family? It would be interesting to know whether this phenomenon is hereditary.

> Sincerely yours,
> Yilmaz Arslan, author of
> *Cats and their Ghosts,*
> (Istanbul, Kirmizi Gül Kitapevi, 1954.)

Yeni Aksham, Istanbul, 18 March 1960, Letter to the Editor, p. 3 of the Weekly Literary and Scientific Supplement.

Dear Sir,

One of the oldest and most honorable members of our association of Shamanistic medical vampires has been authorized by us to treat your correspondent Miss Djevrieh Holivutlu as a charity patient and solely in order to demonstrate the usefulness and efficacity of our art. But she must first sign a notarized statement to the effect that she is willingly allowing herself to be used as a test case for scientific purposes and will make no claims on us should the experiment fail to give the desired results.

> Sincerely yours,
> Tchinghiz Hulaghuoglu

Yeni Aksham, Istanbul, 25 March 1960, Letter to the Editor, p. 3 of the Weekly Literary and Scientific Supplement.

Dear Sir,

You sent me a disgusting old fraud who claimed to be a member in good standing of the National Shamanistic Order of Pan-Turanian Vampires. I am now writing to warn your readers against him. Not only was his treatment painful, humiliating, and quite useless, but I now have a scar that is recognizably that of a vicious human bite further disfiguring my already swollen left buttock. Instead of curing me, his treatment leaves me worse off than I was before.

Sincerely yours,
Djevrieh Holivutlu

Yeni Aksham, Istanbul, 1 April 1960, Letter to the Editor, p. 3 of the Weekly Literary and Scientific Supplement.

Dear Sir,

As President of the Pan-Turanian Association of Shamanistic Vampires I must protest against your irresponsible publication of Miss Djevrieh Holivutlu's absurd and vicious allegations.

She had previously signed a notarized statement, as requested, to the effect that she willingly allowed herself to be used as a test case in a scientific experiment and would make no claims if it failed to produce the desired results. As an eye witness, I must now state that she did not behave, during the experiment, with the proper scientific objectivity. Instead of keeping her composure, she giggled, wriggled, and squealed, so that it was almost impossible for our distinguished member to draw blood from the affected buttock. After the experiment, she even had the effrontery to demand a fee, thus revealing that she believed she was engaging in some curious form of prostitution. Finally, if anyone now has a right to complain, it would surely be our distinguished member who, in his devotion to our venerable science, lost a tooth while trying to treat, free of charge, a silly and immoral woman who refused, as requested, to keep still while he was treating her. Throughout the experiment, she indeed behaved as if she were merely displaying her charms to her customary waterfront audience in a low Tophane café.

Sincerely yours,
Tchinghiz Hulaghuoglu

Yeni Aksham, Istanbul, 1 April 1960, Letter to the Editor, same page as the preceding one.

Dear Sir,

My wife and I are much disturbed by the articles and letters you have published about the Fener vampires and about the plague of vampirism that threatens our children. As parents of five growing boys, we feel that everything should be done to protect the health and morals of those on whose shoulders rests the future of our nation. As for me, if I should ever chance to meet one of these vile and subversive vampires, I would tear him or her apart, regardless of age or sex, limb from limb with my own unarmed hands, then gladly lap up the blood and chew the liver of such a satanic creature. Any other fate would be too good for one of these monsters and I'm sure all other patriotic Turkish parents will agree with me. Long live our glorious Republic.

Alp Karagöz

Yeni Aksham, Istanbul, 1 April 1960, Letter to the Editor, same page as the preceding one.

Dear Sir,

I appeal to your kindness and to the mercy of your readers. Because I have never learned to read or write, I paid the writer in our neighborhood market in Fener to write this letter to all of you, from the widowed mother of the carter Mahmut Osmano-

180

glu who was arrested over a month ago and accused of being a vampire. All my neighbors in Fener know what a good son he has always been, a devout Moslem and kind to all boys and cats in our neighborhood. People have read to me articles and letters you print and I can swear to you on all the Holy Writings of Our Prophet that my son has never stolen and eaten any cats nor does he drink the blood of any boys.

My husband was killed fighting rebel Kurds in the army. A few months later my son was born and never knew his father. We were starving in Edirne and I came to Istanbul with my baby to find work. Many years, I worked all day and half the night in a laundry till I thought I would break my back. Then my boy grew up and went to work and he is a good boy and lets me stay at home and says to me: Mother, you have worked long enough. After that he worked and we both lived on his pay.

Like many other sons who have never known their father my boy is devoted to his mother and has little use for the silly girls of today who think only of movies and gossip. But he has a good heart and would be a wonderful father. All the boys in our neighborhood know him. In summer he takes them to the beach on Sundays and teaches them to swim. In winter he teaches them useful things like how to mend a leaking roof or how to mend their own shoes.

This whole vampire business started when I was away visiting my sister in Edirne. A silly mother in our neighborhood then accused my son of drinking her son's blood. The truth of it is that this evil boy and his two companions are vampires. They came to our lodgings while I was away and threatened to denounce my son to the police if he didn't give them all his week's pay. They said he had taught them to smoke hashish with him in the vacant lot behind the ruins of the old Koranic school in the next street but that isn't true because my son never smokes hashish or even tobacco. After my son was arrested these three boys could no longer agree among themselves what they had accused my son of doing with them. One of them still says he is a vampire and drank their blood but the other boys say nothing. But

181

these three boys are real vampires and you need only see my son now to know that they have been sucking his blood.

Yesterday I was allowed to visit my son for the first time in prison. Every day the police beat him and he now looks like a ghost. Believe me the real vampires are these lying boys and of course the police too. I'm only an old woman but I know a vampire when I see one and they don't suck blood, they drive good men like my son to despair and to their death. What we need now in Turkey is a Caliph like King Solomon to render justice to the poor from his emerald and ruby throne. May God bless you if you print my letter.

Fatima Osmanoglu

Yeni Aksham, Istanbul, 1 April 1960, Letter to the Editor, same page as the preceding one.

Dear Sir,

Vampires, schmampires. Each time I read your newspaper I'm more ashamed of being a Turk. For well over a month, you have now been feeding us hair-raising stories about vampires attacking our children of both sexes. Then you published yesterday a front-page editorial describing how the deputies of the Government party, in our National Parliament in Ankara, had attacked the deputies of the Opposition in a violent free-for-all in the course of which they tore the furniture of the House of Representatives apart and beat each other with the remains of their seats. Such behavior disgraces our nation's politicians in the eyes of the civilized world. The only vampires that we have in Turkey are our politicians of both parties.

As long as you could recognize the Jews, the Armenians, the Greeks, or the Shiah Moslems in our midst by their headdresses, we used to have massacres whenever our tempers rose to boiling point. Now we all wear more or less the same hats and massacre each other at random. The only solution to this problem of Turkish national unity would be to allow only two kinds of hat

182

in Turkey: one hat for the sadists and another hat for the masochists, and no hat at all for the majority of neutrals. Tit for tat and hit for hat, everybody would then be happy, the sadists beating up the masochists and the masochists being merrily beaten up by the sadists with no complaints later, while the rest of us would go about our daily business in peace or sit back and applaud the massacre like a football match in the Beziktash Stadium.

Perhaps we need to be psychoanalyzed as a nation. We're all too bloodthirsty, all of us vampires at heart. It may be useful to be bloodthirsty in times of war, but we're a failure in peacetime as a democratic nation. As for me, I've made my choice and become a vegetarian. If all Turks could only shift their attention from blood to chlorophyll, we might become a civilized nation within a couple of generations. Boys and girls would then be safe in our midst, but God protect a cabbage when I'm around! Vegetables already tremble when they see me approach them.

Sincerely yours,
Harun Pezevenkoglu

Yeni Aksham, Istanbul, 4 September 1960, p. 3 local news.

Our readers will remember that, six months ago, *Yeni Aksham* was the only daily newspaper in Istanbul to denounce as nonsense, from the very start, the absurd panic caused in our city by entirely unfounded rumors of vampirism. Thanks to our enlightened campaign, the innocent victim of this malicious gossip was finally proven to be no vampire and was released from prison.

But the press of other nations appears to be more credulous than ours. Foreign news agencies thus distributed to American newspapers distorted versions of our published reports of the investigation of the case of the alleged vampires of Fener. Thanks to our courageous press campaign, the carter Mahmut Osmanoglu, the only alleged vampire who had been arrested, has now been a free man again for many months. He was working peacefully at his old job as a carter, willing to forgive and forget, when he suddenly received two weeks ago a letter from America. After reading in the American press its somewhat sensational reports of alleged Turkish vampirism, an American research institute was offering Mahmut Osmanoglu a generous grant to come to America and co-operate there with a group of scientists on an important project to determine the physical and psychological causes of both hereditary and environmental vampirism. Yesterday morning, Mahmut Osmanoglu, accompanied by his aged mother, left Yesilköy airport for Chicago, where he will henceforth work as a kind of piece of human litmus paper to detect, by his reactions, who is a potential vampire and who is not.

Our reporter interviewed Mahmut Osmanoglu at the airport, a few minutes before he boarded the plane. A man of few words, he declared only that he plans to spend much of his spare time in Chicago as a voluntary missionary to convert Americans to Islam. "I've been told," he declared, "that most of them live on a diet of pork and whisky, though they would actually prefer to suck the blood of Communists. Every once in a while, however, they are obliged to send some of their more bloodthirsty vampires on raids to Cuba, San Domingo, or Vietnam to suck the blood of Communists as they no longer have enough of them at home. It was high time I went to America to wean them away from their unclean diet and their propensity for political cannibalism."

Mahmut Osmanoglu's mission to America can thus be interpreted as Turkey's first attempt at technical assistance to an overdeveloped nation. We may soon expect other such idealistic Turkish pioneers to leave our country on similar UNESCO-sponsored projects to solve the problems of France, Western Germany, Sweden, Switzerland, and the United Kingdom, nations which are equally infested, it seems, with the kind of vampirism that develops all too easily in an economy of leisure and plenty.

184